The Seeds of Hope Devotional

"May the God of peace fill you with all joy
and peace as you trust in him"

Kate Carroll

Self-published

ISBN:9798779190183

Forever grateful to my friend, the great encourager Frank Cairns. Your simple request to share words of hope with our prayer group was the first seed for this devotional. Sorry you missed seeing it in print.

TABLE OF CONTENTS

47: *Courage is Contagious* – Take courage
48: *Treading water* – Don't panic
49: *Blinkers on* – Staying focused
50: *Ease of passage* – Hard times
51: *Second chances* – God's mercy
52: *Cultivating Friendships* – Friendship
53: *Clouds overhead* – Our refuge
54: *Time up* – Procrastination
55: *Take shelter* - Shielded from harm
56: *Still producing fruit* – Wisdom which comes with age
57: *Pulled the short straw* – Rejoicing with others
58: *Pulled the short straw* – Rejoicing with others
59: *Heritage from the Lord* - Children are a blessing
60: *Not a dress rehearsal* -The real thing
61: *Pity Vs Compassion*
62: *Replenish* – Spending time with God
63: *Piggy back* – Help from our Father
64: *Special care units* - New Christians
65: *Jump start* –Help one another
66: *On average* – choosing our words carefully
67: *Perhaps* – Meditating on the word of God
68: *Room to grow* – Embracing the new
69: *The pinata* - Don't quit praying
70: *Lead by example* – Train up a child
71: *Drifting* - Anchoring our minds
72: *Toothpaste tube* - Keep going
73: *By name* – Name not a number
74: *Elephant Ears* - Gossip
75: *Be prepared* – Salvation
76: *Is it, or isn't it?* -Thoughts
77: *Excuses, Excuses* - Obeying the promptings
78: *All your might* – Diligence
79: *Morning has Broken* - Thankful for today
80: *Overpayment* - Forgiveness
81: *Saver or Spender?* – Use your gifts
82: *In comparison to* - Sin
83: *Shattered* – Brokenness
84: *Even the Spanish Ants* - Seeking Him
85: *Let's not wallow* - Self-pity
86: *A Promise* – Faith
87: *The Ripple Effect* - Our actions
88: *Smudge Marks* – Hold fast to truth
89: *Precious pearls* – Fixing
90: *The real deal* –Truth
91: *Strengthened from within* – Rejoicing in hope
92: *Fail better* – Getting back up
93: *Fail better* – Getting back up
94: *Laced up* – Bringing together
95: *Corresponding actions* - Love softens
96: *Derailed by disappointment* – Back on the tracks

Did I? Do I? Will I? - Obeying the word

A portion of Joshua 1v8 was playing in my head and I started to mull over it, thinking about meditating on the word of God. I decided this was the chosen scripture to encourage my family with, God's recipe for success. I was focusing on the meditating part but before I pressed the send button, a portion of the scripture jumped out at me "that you may observe to do."

We can ask ourselves this question "do I do everything written in the word?" I am sure most of us would like success and for our way to be prosperous. But are we doing all that is written therein?

Are there verses in the bible that make us squirm? Is there something that makes us feel uncomfortable? Do we skip over certain passages or have we reassured ourselves that certain matters don't apply to us? Do we let ourselves off the hook in an area because for the most part we are doing what is written therein? Have we convinced ourselves that certain things no longer apply or are relevant for the times we are living in? Did I, do I, will I?

Joshua 1v8

"This Book of the Law shall not depart from your mouth, but you shall meditate in it day and night, that you may observe to do according to all that is written in it. For then you will make your way prosperous, and then you will have good success"

Father help me today to not only keep the word of God in my mouth, to not only meditate on it but also to observe to do all that is written therein.

"She never gave up on me" - The prodigal

I listened to the words which flowed like honey at a friend's memorial service. People didn't have to dig deep to find things to say, such was the measure of the lady who oozed love, bubbled over with joy, served tirelessly and gave of herself to others in so many ways. One of the many "responsibility hats" hanging in her wardrobe was for the children's ministry in her church.

A video was played of the children being asked questions about their beloved leader. Six words jumped out at me, spoken by a young boy.

"She never gave up on me."

And I thought, just like our Heavenly Father with each one of us. We might have blown it; we may have blown it more times than we can even count. Others may have given up on us. We may have given up on ourselves. But our Heavenly Father never has and never will give up on us. No matter how far we may have run from Him or how deep we may have fallen.

While yet still a long way off, He stands looking, waiting, ready, arms outstretched, longing to welcome the prodigal home again.

Luke 15v21

"But while he was still a long way off, his father saw him and was filled with compassion for him; he ran to his son, threw his arms around him and kissed him"

So, let's not let fear, allow shame or guilt, entertain pride or anything that could stop us taking the first step towards home.

Luke 15v22-24

"But the father said to his servants, 'Quick! Bring the best robe and put it on him. Put a ring on his finger and sandals on his feet. Bring the fattened calf and kill it. Let's have a feast and celebrate. For this son of mine was dead and is alive again; he was lost and is found.' So, they began to celebrate"

We pray for the prodigals today. We pray for changes of hearts, changes in direction and that today will begin their journey home towards their Father. For those of us with prodigals, help us to never stop loving, never stop praying, never stop trusting and to be ready to celebrate when they make the journey home. If you are a prodigal, remember you are never too far and it's never too late to return to your heavenly Father.

Access Denied - Salvation

I am sure we can all relate to the feelings that come when we have lost or misplaced something. In my opinion there is something that is harder than other things to lose. For we can borrow money if a wallet is lost, tinfoil can replace a missing lid, odd socks will do when in a rush, someone else's mobile phone can be used to make contact when our phone is hiding. But when our house keys are missing and we are outside of the property, we are locked out.

A passer-by's key won't work, a friend's key won't fit, no matter how helpful a team mate is, his house key is no good. Only our uniquely cut key will allow us to gain entry. Even in an apartment with shared access codes to communal areas, each resident must have their unique key to open their front door.

John 14v6

"I am the way, the truth and the life. No one comes to the Father except by me"

In many situations we can improvise. In others we can get help. However, no amount of neighbour's keys can get me through my locked front door, no witty ideas can get me in and no amount of physical strength can get the wrong key to turn in my lock.

Jesus is the one way and the only way to heaven. No matter how many great inventions have still to be thought up or how far society progresses or what new ideas are come up with. John 14v6 will always stand. He is the way, the truth and the life and no one can come to the Father except through Him. Without Jesus, access is denied.

Father thank You for sending Your son, Jesus, who is the way, the truth and the life. Thank You for the promise in Romans 10v13, that anyone who calls on the name of the Lord will be saved. Thank You that with Jesus, access is not denied.

Out of the rubble - Grief

A crowd stood watching the giant wrecking ball dangling from the crane. The old Dublin building was fast being reduced to a pile of rubble. And I wondered about the buildings story and those who had used it over the years. Ash in the grate, rubble on a building site or a ruin on the horizon all speak of - what has been, what used to be, what was and what is no more.

Isaiah 61v3

"To bestow on them a crown of beauty instead of ashes, the oil of joy instead of mourning, and a garment of praise instead of a spirit of despair"

The emotion of grief is not solely reserved for the loss of a loved one through death. We can experience grief over a relationship that has ended, a ministry we are no longer involved in, a stage of life that has come to an end, a business that had to close. We can grieve for the working life when retirement starts or our children when the nest empties.

Grief hurts. Grief is a process. The fire grate will be cleaned out and a fresh fire laid. The rubble on the Dublin building site didn't lie there as a permanent reminder of what once was but was cleared away. I walked past the demolition site again recently and the empty space left by the demolition has been filled. Work on a new motel is well under way, out of the rubble, out of the emptiness, building has begun and a new purpose has been found for this site.

Isaiah 43v19

"See, I am doing a new thing! Now it springs up; do you not perceive it? I am making a way in the wilderness and streams in the wasteland"

Father help all who are grieving today. Give them the strength and courage when the time is right to clear the ash from the grate, to remove the rubble from the site, to make way for the new. Strengthen them to lay fresh kindling in the grate or to start the brickwork for the new build. Help them while grateful for the "old" to be excited about the "new". Thank You for beauty instead of ashes, oil of joy instead of mourning and for the garment of praise instead of a spirit of despair.

Caught off Guard – Our refuge

Sometimes beach goers have got caught off guard when walking a beach, they were not familiar with. The tide way out when they set off, they walked along the shoreline at ease. They turned to retrace their steps only to discover a different scenario.

Their route back has become blocked by rising sea water, the tide has turned. Where there was a path before them is now fast approaching water.

Have you ever been caught off guard when the tide has turned? Have you ever looked and all you can see is water and you struggle to find a dry patch on which to step? You cannot see a way through or a way forward and you think what now?

The beach goer found a rock, a rock that they scaled. A rock that was higher than the rising tide, a rock which led to safety and solid ground on which to walk.

When facing a sea of circumstances too deep to wade through we have a rock to climb onto to, a rock to cling to. A rock higher than the water of circumstances, a rock that won't dissolve in the sea of troubles, a rock strong enough to withstand the bashing waves. A rock still standing even after being hit by an unexpected, freak wave.

Psalm 61v2&3

"From the ends of the earth I call to you, I call as my heart grows faint; lead me to the rock that is higher than I. For you have been my refuge, a strong tower against the foe"

Father when I need refuge and a strong tower, please lead me to the rock that is higher than I.

In season – Knowing the season

I have fond memories of Granny's Garden and vegetable garden. Picking and shelling peas, walking between the raspberry canes hoping to find the ripe berries before the birds feasted on them. Blackcurrant bushes heavy with their crop. The smell of ripening tomatoes in her greenhouse. I learnt the hard way, fruit is best left on branches and vines until fully ripe after helping myself to handfuls of hard, unripe gooseberries. It wasn't yet "their season". In times past the only fruit and vegetables available to buy were those that were "in season". Eating fruit and vegetables that are "in season" have greater flavour and are more nutritious.

If I'd waited, leaving the gooseberries on the bush, they would've been harvested at the right time and turned into gooseberry fool or jam. I moved too early. Granny knew when to sow, she knew how to care for what was sown and she knew how to wait. She knew when it was time to pull on her green wellingtons, pick up her spade and turn the soil to find the potatoes which had grown beneath ground. She knew the correct time to pull up the carrots, snip the head off lettuce, fill her basin with juicy ripe berries. She knew the seasons. Many of us have sown seed, seeds of hope, dream seeds, seeds of faith, financial seeds, seeds of prayer and at times we feel like making a move and yet the whisper from above is "in season". Some of us have big dreams and exciting plans and frustration can come when it appears as if nothing is happening. Like repeatedly looking at a plan on an architect's board or screen when we want to see it become a reality. Our passion, enthusiasm and drive are bubbling over and yet the whisper from above is "in season". If I had waited until we came back from the trip to France, those gooseberries would have been tasty and ripe.

Perhaps He is directing some today to wait a little longer, press in a little deeper, persevere for a while more, pray with greater fervency, to keep trusting and keep watching for the green light of release and for the sound of the words "in season." The produce from Granny's Garden not only blessed her but others it was given to as an ingredient or a component of something she had made, cooked or baked.

Ecclesiastes 3v1

"To everything there is a season, and a time to every purpose under the heaven"

Father help me to know and discern the seasons. Help me to know if I am in a season of sowing, watering or harvesting. Help me to stay "in season".

How much is too much? - God's love

The excitement was tangible, coming over the airwaves. The Irish lady being interviewed living in Australia now sees hope at the end of the tunnel of separation. An expected time frame has been given for the Australian borders to begin reopening after being closed due to the pandemic. She can now come home. The all-important question was then put to her. How much do flights home cost?

With some of my loved ones living in Australia I'm well aware of the distance between us. This has now been compounded by lockdowns, travel restrictions and border closures. So, I pondered on the question, how much is too much to pay to be reunited? How much to no longer be separated from loved ones?

Out of the car window at Dublin airport recently, I spotted a young returning traveller. "Momma, Momma, Momma" she called. In my wing mirror I could see Momma, making her way towards her daughter, arms outstretched as she shouted back. They met, embraced, held each other and didn't let go. How much is too much to pay to no longer be separated?

John 3v16

"For God so loved the world that He gave his one and only Son, that whoever believes in him shall not perish but shall have everlasting life"

We were separated from God because of sin.

John 3v3

 "Jesus answered and said unto him, "Verily, verily, I say unto thee, except a man be born again, he cannot see the kingdom of God"

 A price was paid to end the separation. That price was His one and only son, Jesus.

1 John 4v9

"God showed how much he loved us by sending his one and only Son into the world so that we might have eternal life through him"

Father thank You for showing Your love for us by sending Your one and only son, to pay the price for our sin so that we no longer would have to be separated.

The Tenner – Resilience

Stuck to the washing machine door was my sons missing ten euro. Wet but still intact after it's stint in the washing machine. No damage done, ready to be spent, to do what it was made to do.

Tissues have at times mistakenly made it into the washing machine concealed like the money in pockets. They have not fared well, coming out shredded into tiny bits, of no further use or benefit to anyone.

Isaiah 43v2

"When you pass through the waters, I will be with you and when you pass through the rivers, they will not sweep over you. When you walk through the fire you will not be burned, the flames will not set you ablaze"

At times the pressures, trials or disappointments can be so great that we wonder will our fate be like that of the tissues in the washing machine causing us to dissolve or fall apart.

Isaiah 43 promises that He is with us when we pass through the waters, no matter how far dry land seems or how high or fast the waters are rising around us. The river of loneliness, sickness, fear, grief, depression, addiction, isolation will not sweep over us. When we walk through the fire, we will not be burned. We may be standing watching the flames get higher, smelling the smoke, listening to the crackle, feeling the heat yet Isaiah 43 promises we will not get burned.

Three times in the above verse, we read the word through. We trust Him today that no matter what water we are going through, or river we are passing through or fire we are going through that we will come out the other side like the tenner, still doing what we were created to do. Still fulfilling purpose.

Father thank You for the promises in Isaiah 43. Thank You for being with me when I pass through the waters. Thank You that you have promised that the rivers will not sweep over me when I pass through them. Thank You that when I walk through the fire, I will not be burned.

My Peace I Give You – His peace

People seek peace in many ways and different places. Holiday destinations are described as "peaceful getaways". Ambiances are created by decor, music, candles, flowing fountains and open fires and yet do all these bring true and lasting peace? What happens when the trip to the spa ends, the luxury holiday is over or you descend from the peaceful mountain top?

Before He was crucified, Jesus told His disciples that He was leaving them but He also told them He was leaving them His peace. He was their friend, their teacher, their guide, mentor and leader. How must they have felt at the thought of Him going?

John 14v27

"Peace I leave with you; my peace I give you. I do not give to you as the world gives. Do not let your hearts be troubled and do not be afraid"

"I do not give as the world gives" So often peace in this world is based on circumstances. What happens when these circumstances change? The peace He gives us is not dependent on our circumstances. It doesn't come and go depending on what we are facing, where we are or whose company, we are in. Therefore, we can have peace even when we face hard and difficult situations, when we are in places, we wish we weren't and when we are with people who we'd rather not be with.

"Do not let your heart be troubled". We are to not let our hearts be troubled and then He says "and do not be afraid." But you might be thinking "easy for you to say, you don't know the landslide I am looking at or the myriad of hard circumstances I am facing"

Philippians 4v6&7 is one of my favourite portions of scripture. No matter how fearful, nervous or frazzled we may feel today, we can heed the advice in these verses and rather than being anxious we can choose to pray instead. In everything by prayer and supplication, with thanksgiving, we can let our requests be made known to God. And when we do, we are promised that the peace of God which surpasses all understanding will guard our hearts and minds in Christ Jesus.

Maybe today hasn't started the way we hoped, anticipated or wanted. We can change course and tactics and if we haven't already done it, take a moment and pray.

Seaview's – Appreciation for others

For two thirds of my life, I lived by the sea in the same part of Dublin. I love the sea and all it offers. Today, enroute somewhere, I took the scenic route through very familiar territory. A beautiful bright, sunny, clear morning and the views were spectacular. I parked and drank in the beauty of My Fathers handiwork. I pondered, when I lived with this on my doorstep, did I stop in awe and wonder every time I passed by? I always appreciated it, but I got accustomed to it "just being there".

There are many who we share our lives with, we have become accustomed to them "just being there" and we can be guilty at times of taking them for granted. There is much about the nation we live in we can overlook and forget to be thankful for. The physical things we have been blessed with; we sometimes don't even see. The gifts and talents He has deposited in us we can take for granted.

Today let's take a virtual drive, wipe the condensation from the windows and admire all the views in our lives. Let's not just admire them but take a minute to thank Him for all He has blessed us with, and all who He has blessed us with in our lives.

When my mother died, we received many letters about her; beautiful, kind words and sentiments. I wondered if she'd been told these things herself over the years? My mother died young, so perhaps people thought there would be plenty of opportunities to tell her what she meant to them. We're great in Ireland at saying lovely things about people when they're no longer around to hear these words. Maybe partly because we Irish traditionally weren't always the best at taking a compliment. I decided after receiving those letters about Mum, to try, when possible, to seize opportunities to sow encouragement to the living.

My dear friend who was the catalyst for this devotional, was reaching his 90th birthday earlier this year so I asked people who he'd been a blessing to, of which there were many, if they'd like to give me a photo of them with him and pen some words. The love and deep appreciation for this great father figure in the body of Christ who had helped so many with his love, encouragement and friendship impacted me as I put his birthday book together. Two months after my friends 90th birthday he went to his heavenly home. I for one was glad that not only was I telling his loved ones (which I did) how much this friend meant to me and my family, but that I had told him himself.

Father help me to not let opportunities slip past to show appreciation for those in my life. Help me not put it off or on the long finger, but to start today sowing seeds of love and appreciation, in Jesus' name.

Clann – Family

The frame got knocked over and the piece of pewter with the word Clann on it, meaning family in Irish fell off. The word Clann now lies haphazardly under the glass frame and rattles around if the frame is moved. Families like my picture, can take knocks making it feel or look like things are haphazard, unsure and unstable.

My white frame is fixable, the exterior can be removed, the little name plaque glued and then held firmly in place until the glue has time to set. After the repairs the frame would appear as "good as new" with only those "in the know" being aware that it's taken a knock.

Perhaps for some reading this there are family relationships that have come apart. They are crying out for some glue and then to be held to give the glue time to set. Maybe hairline cracks have appeared in relationship walls which if left untreated, don't just disappear but unfortunately tend to widen. Oft times when warning bells are ignored, the repairs required are not only greater but more costly.

While we may be tempted to simply gloss over situations and issues, sometimes before we can bring about the new, some of the old needs dealing with. The old flaky paint in a relationship needs to be scrapped away before the new coat of paint applied. Rotten timber needs removing before it can be replaced. Old wallpaper needs to be steamed off before the new wallpaper can be hung.

1 Corinthians 13V5

"Love keeps no record of wrongs"

What carpenter keeps rotten timber? The old wallpaper that has been peeled off or the scrapings of paint are binned not held onto. So too when things have been sorted and resolved with family members, we would be best advised to let go of the old and embrace the new.

Ephesians 4v2

"Be completely humble and gentle; be patient, bearing with one another in love"

Father, please fix damaged, broken family relationships. Those with hairline cracks, those hanging on by a thread and even those that look irreparable such is the void that lies between the parties. Please give wisdom what practical steps can be taken. During the healing process help the parties involved to remain humble and patient, to be gentle while bearing with one another in love. When the matter has been resolved please help there be no record of wrongs kept.

Betwixt and Between – Decision making

Have you ever observed a small child trying to decide between two options? Should it be the chocolate sauce drizzled on their ice cream or rainbow sprinkles tossed on top? Should Mary be the tenth person on their birthday list as they went to her party when in reality, they want to invite Susie, who is so much more fun? Often times they reason aloud, the pros and cons of each choice and what the potential outcomes will be.

Have you ever felt betwixt and between two options? It can seem like the choices are hanging before you on an old-fashioned weighing scales. At times choice A is the weightier one but then with further consideration it is choice B, but hang on choice A seems to be getting heavier again.

While sauce over sprinkles is not really a life changing choice, many times the choices we make have far greater consequences. At times we face crossroad moments, should we go left or will we hang right? Looking at the weighing scales or standing at the crossroads can cause stress, anxious thoughts, interrupted sleep and can affect one's mood. Being "betwixt and between" oft times is not a pleasant place to be.

Proverbs 3v5&6

"Trust in the LORD with all your heart, and lean not on your own understanding; in all your ways acknowledge him, and he shall direct your paths"

I love this bible passage. When we trust Him completely with all of our heart, when we don't try and figure things out by leaning on our own understanding, when we acknowledge Him in all of our ways. Then we have a promise that He will direct our paths. No longer will we have to deal with all that uncertainty brings, no more tossing and turning at night fearing we are making a wrong choice. The big "what ifs" are erased, because He promises to direct our paths. Today simply trust, lean, acknowledge and let Him do the guiding, leading and directing.

Father help me if I am betwixt and between and finding it hard to choose or to make a decision. Help me to trust You completely, to not try to figure it all out but rather to acknowledge You in all my ways and You have promised that You will direct my paths.

In a name - I am who I am

A friend of a similar age to me declared recently that she doesn't hear children called by her name as it's gone out of fashion. Lists are published annually of the current most popular boys' and girls' names. Children are often named after family members, famous people or a characteur from a novel. How often do we choose a name not because we like it's sound but because of its' meaning? I love to hear my Nigerian friends explain the meanings of their carefully chosen names. When Moses encountered God at the burning bush, he asked "Suppose I go to the Israelites and say to them, 'The God of your fathers has sent me to you,' and they ask me, 'What is his name?' Then what shall I tell them?" and God replied "I am who I am."

He is our Abba Father (Mark 14v36), not a distant hierarchical figure but our Father. If we feel overlooked, invisible, forgotten or forsaken, He is El Roi which means the God who sees. He sees even when it feels like no one around us does. He sees the situations we face; He knows the paths we have already walked; He knows the things we are ashamed to tell another, He saw the hurts that were inflicted on us, He knows our most intimate thoughts, He is El Roi.

If we feel forsaken, abandoned and alone today. Yahweh – Shammah is with us.

Ezekiel 48v35

"The Lord is present"

He not only sees but He is present. He will never leave us, walk out on us, desert us, turn away from us, reject us, replace us, dump us for another or abandon us. He is Yahweh – Shammah.

Father thank You that you are my Abba Father today, my Daddy whom I can run to. Thank You that you are El Roi, the God who sees. Thank You that you are Yahweh – Shammah, the God who is with me, whom I can trust to never leave me, and thank You, that you are so much more. You are Yahweh – Jireh the Lord who will provide, You are Yahweh – Rapha the Lord who heals, You are Jehovah Shalom, the Lord our peace.

13

One more toss – Casting your cares

We went on a museum visit to one crammed with Irish history. When we were leaving the little boy with us wanted to prolong his visit, not to see another exhibit or to revisit the coffee shop. Rather he wanted to have "one more toss". For he was enjoying throwing stones into a puddle in the museum's car park.

I stood beside rock pools last weekend enjoying the beauty of the scenery around me. I paused to pick up, then throw some stones into the rock pools. There is something liberating about releasing the stones, watching them hit the water and the splash which then follows.

Some of us may need to make some splashes today. Perhaps we are carrying a heavy weight which is not only weighing us down but also slowing us down. Have you ever lugged a load too heavy for too long, it doesn't only take a toll physically, it can also start to affect your mood?

For some perhaps it is not one gigantic rock weighing you down but rather it feels like you have pockets full of pebbles. Pretty as they are, pockets full of pebbles will start to drag you down.

1 Peter 5v7

"Cast all your anxiety on him, for he cares for you"

"God cares for you so turn all your worries over to him" is how another version puts it while another says "leave all your worry with him" or "throw all your worry unto him" is how the international standard version puts it.

Today let's lighten our load of any unwanted rocks, let's search pockets and shoes for any pebbles that don't need to be there. One big rock hitting the water makes a big splash but equally lots of little pebbles makes a big impact on the water.

Happy throwing, casting and chucking today of any worries, cares, concerns or anxieties over to Him.

Father thank You that You care for me and that I can turn my worries over to You. Today I choose to cast all my cares on You and help me to not try and take them back, in Jesus' name.

Courage – Take courage

Courage is defined as the ability to do something that frightens one. Strength in the face of pain or grief.

1 Corinthians 16v13

"Be on your guard, stand firm in the faith, be courageous be strong"

You may feel like the person about to do a sky dive. Feeling terrified as they look out the door of the plane despite the parachute on their back. Perhaps you are standing ready to take a leap of faith, or a leap into the unknown not with a parachute on your back, but rather with Him at your back. The parachute for the sky diver is only opened once they have taken the leap and left the security of the plane.

Maybe you are facing a painful circumstance, feeling alone and scared and He is whispering, take courage, I am with you, I will never leave you or forsake you, and though circumstances change, I am the God who changes not - Malachi 3v6

Deuteronomy 31v6

"Be strong and courageous. Do not be afraid or terrified because of them, for the Lord God goes with you he will never leave you nor forsake you"

Whatever you might be facing today - a new job that you wonder are you equipped for, a move to a new area or country, a child about to leave the nest, a medical diagnosis, a court case, separation, an exam, a relationship breaks up or another situation. We can be strong and courageous knowing that the Lord God goes with us. He will not leave us nor forsake us, and while circumstances may change, He is the God who changes not.

Father help me to be courageous, help me to have the ability to do something even that may frighten me in the natural. When facing painful situations help me to be courageous. Help me to remember that You are here with me every step of the way and have promised to never leave me nor forsake me. It is in You I put my trust today.

The Best Thing You Can Do - After I pray

"The best thing you can do for your kids is to stay at the feet of Jesus." Words spoken by the worship leader on Sunday morning after he made reference to Martha and Mary. I reflected how I pray for my children, have people who agree with me in prayer for them, use scripture prayer books to pray into different situations for my young adult children. I am blessed to have friends I walk with and as we do, we lift up our children in prayer. But what then? What next?

After praying for my children, after speaking the word of God over them, after praying with others for them, do I then stay at the feet of Jesus?

At His feet He works in us. At His feet we are filled up. At His feet there's no distractions so we can hear clearly from Him. At His feet we are not worrying, nagging, or fretting over our children.

Sound advice no matter where on the parenting journey we are. Navigating the first steps, in the middle of the road, watching our children get ready to fly the coop or perhaps our offspring are long physically left home, some even now themselves on the parenting journey. Yet we never stop praying for our children and for that which concerns them.

In as much as this applies to our physical children, so too with our spiritual children. Those whom we have loved, whom we have prayed for, discipled and at times even disciplined as a parent would a child in the natural.

Martha was busy when Jesus came to visit their home but Mary chose the better way and remained at His feet.

Father help me after I have prayed, after I have cast the cares, after I have entrusted issues, after I have asked for wisdom in different situations, to not get busy trying to fix and to sort out but rather remain at Your feet. Help me not to interfere, worry, nag or fret but rather to trust and entrust my physical and spiritual children to you. In Jesus name I pray.

Crockery – Vessels of God

My mother-in-law likes to drink her tea from a thin mug. I love visiting my Kilkenny friends and being served my tea out of a Mosse pottery mug.

Some like tea in a mug, some prefer a cup and saucer while others won't entertain tea except from a paper cup.

Same tea but different crockery. I don't like drinking tea from a paper cup and before it even reaches my lips, I have decided I won't like the taste. I have judged the contents on the vessel serving it.

We are served the word of God by many different vessels. At times like me with tea from a paper cup, we have decided before a word is spoken by the teacher or preacher or we have read a word they have written - that it's not to our taste.

Our focus can be on the vessel rather than the contents and thus miss the message. Tea is tea no matter what vessel it is served in.

Have we at times missed the message that God wants us to hear because our focus has been on the messenger rather than the message?

The vessels style of preaching is not to our taste. The vessels accent grates on us. What could they have to say that we haven't already heard? The vessel is only a new Christian. We judge the vessel on their race, age or ethnicity. The vessel said something in the past that we didn't agree with. So, we close our ears or our eyes and miss the message.

Father help me to be led by the Spirit what to read and what to listen to rather than being dictated to by the vessel that brings the message. Father show me if because of prejudices I have missed out on things You wanted me to hear. I am sorry for vessel judging.

Keep the hand brake on – **The Mercy of God**

Sitting in our parked car on Patrick's Street in Dunlaoire as children, my brother released the handbrake. The car parked behind ours put an end to the cars, backward, descent.

A handbrake keeps the vehicle in position and stops it rolling. I wonder how far down the hill towards the Irish Sea we would have gone if not stopped in our tracks? It's much easier to prevent a vehicle from moving by applying the handbrake than to have to attempt to stop a rolling vehicle when the driver's seat is empty.

How often have we thought when observing the damage caused "if only I hadn't taken the handbrake off my tongue"? Or if only I could back track to when I released the handbrake and did something against my better judgement. That release setting in place a chain of undesirable circumstances.

Father I repent for those times when I have released the handbrake knowingly when I knew I shouldn't. Please forgive me.

When a rolling vehicle causes damage, the damages have to be paid for.

Father make us aware of any pain or damage we have caused others by releasing the handbrake when we shouldn't. Help us where possible to make restitution or to make right for any damage caused by our words, actions or choices.

Lord, thank You that Your steadfast love never ceases. Thank You that Your mercies are new every morning for great is Your faithfulness. Thank You that though a righteous man falls seven times, he gets back up. Thank You for the strength and courage to get back up and continue on my journey.

Entrust – Give it to God

Something was on my mind. I heard the whisper of God. One simple word "Entrust" I was to entrust this situation to Him.

The definition of entrust is to "assign the responsibility for doing something to someone" or "to put something into someone's care or protection."

We all probably have things, people and situations that we are praying for and about. Things we are trusting God with. If someone asked us, we would probably declare "I am trusting God".

Psalm 31v14

"But I trust in you O Lord"

Jeremiah 17v7

"Blessed is the one who trusts in the Lord, whose confidence is in him"

However, while we are trusting Him, are there situations, people or relationships, that we need to entrust to God?

People bring their precious jewels and gold, their wealth to the bank and entrust the bank to take care of it. At other times we bring broken things to be mended and we entrust them to the care of the experts to fix.

Perhaps you are like me praying fervently about a situation and God is whispering "entrust". Hand the situation over to Me to take of care of it, leave the responsibility for sorting it out to Me.

He is not going to grab it out of our hands neither is He going to prise it from our clenched first, He simply waits for us to release it to Him.

Father, please shine the spotlight on any area of my life that I need to entrust to You today. Help me to give the situation, relationship or the person into Your capable hands. Thank you for the release that comes with entrusting.

As the crow flies – Time it takes

As I walked in the grounds of Maynooth college at the end of Spring, I noticed a new path had been cut out in the grass. The grass path runs alongside the permanent tarmac path with both paths starting and ending in the same place. When planning a physical journey if we could go the route "that the crow flies" it would be the quickest and shortest. This route is usually not a possibility.

I considered a situation that a member of my family was walking through. While I would have liked for them to be on the straight tarmac path, their path was the twisty grass one. The grass grew over the summer, visibility on the grass path was reduced making it harder to see the end destination.

Perhaps some of us can relate to the twisty grass path, we know where we are headed but it seems to be taking longer than expected and our journey has had more twists and turns than we anticipated when we started out. In life when we plan for the straight path, dream of the straight path and yet find ourselves on a twisty one, we can be tempted to give up on our journey.

We can see people who started at the same time as us reach their destination quickly as they journeyed on the tarmac path and even ones who started long after us are overtaking us on the tarmac path. Autumn came and the family member made it to their destination by the Grace of God, and I said a prayer of thanks.

I would like to encourage anyone on the twisty grass path who feels like quitting, throwing in the towel or giving up. It may take a little longer, it may require greater resolve and resilience, it may require more faith but don't quit just because the path has more twists and turns than the straight tarmac one.

The God of the straight tarmac path is also the God of the twisty path.

Matthew 19v26

"Jesus looked at them and said, "With man this is impossible, but with God all things are possible"

Father help me when I find myself on a twisty, grass path that I can't see the end of, because of all the turns. Help me to keep trusting You and to keep going, even when I may feel like leaving the path.

End of one's tether – **Feel like giving up**

A grazing animal at times is tethered by a rope to a stake in the ground, when he gets to the end of the tether it means there is no more rope. Perhaps we have used the expression "I am at the end of my tether" referring to a situation or a person's behaviour.

It means to be at the end of one's patience, strength or endurance. "I have tried everything, yet nothing has worked and I am now at the end of my tether". "We are at the end of our tether dealing with our child's behaviour". "I am at the end of my tether with this work situation." "This legal matter has rumbled on for so long that I find myself at the end of my tether."

When we feel like we have no further strength in an area or multiple areas, we can take heart from Psalm 18.

Psalm 18v1

"I love you Lord, my strength"

In chapter 32 of the same Psalm, it says "it is God who arms me with strength"

Psalm 18v16&17

"He reached down from on high and took hold of me, he drew me out of deep waters. He rescued me from my powerful enemy. From my foes who were too strong for me"

I love that image of God reaching down, taking hold of me, drawing me out of deep waters and rescuing me from enemies, that were too strong for me but not for Him. Verse 19 says He rescued me because He delighted in me.

Father help me to remember when I reach the end of the rope and feel at the end of my tether, that You are my strength, my shield, my help, my rescuer.

Exodus 14v14

"The Lord will fight for you. You only need to be still."

Slow down – Speed of life

If a snail and a cheetah were in a race, the latter would no doubt cross the finish line first but would the former have gained more from the experience?

I have walked routes that I have traversed multiple times in a car, and suddenly I find myself noticing and seeing things for the first time. Little details missed when I drove past.

Pacemakers are used in some long-distance races to set the pace, often so a record can be smashed by a competitor in the race. The pace setters in the game of life now run so much quicker than those who ran in previous decades. There is a cry in the air which shouts, "faster, faster" and yet as we race like the cheetah through life, we risk missing what the snail is enjoying along the route.

When Timothy talks about finishing his race, he never referred to the speed he completed it in, there is no claim to having run at bottle neck speed. A lit match will eventually burn out. All of us need to refuel and often times there is no other way than by pulling the brakes, stopping and taking time to rest.

Genesis 2v2

"By the seventh day God had finished the work he had been doing so on the seventh day he rested from all His work"

We can learn and follow in His footsteps. In Matthew 11, He promises rest to those who are labouring and feeling heavy burden.

Psalm 37v7

"Be still before the Lord and wait patiently for Him"

Thank You Lord for Your leading and guiding today and in this season. Thank You for being my pacemaker, if You are whispering "move" I will up the pace but if You are directing me to "slow down" I will pull the brakes and rest awhile.

Half full or half empty? - Contentment

We have all no doubt heard or used the analogy about the person looking at the glass of liquid. Do they call the glass "half full" or do they call it "half empty?" Two people looking at the same glass, can choose to see it and call it differently. Sometimes, all of our attention and focus can be on the empty top half of the glass, rather than the full bottom half. There is a misconception that once the glass is full, that then "everything will be alright" and our contentment will be at 100 percent.

Philippians 4v11&12

"For I have learned to be content whatever the circumstances. I know what it is to be in need and I know what it is to have plenty. I have learned the secret of being content in any and every situation"

We can learn like the apostle Paul to be content in every situation. It's a choice to be grateful rather than a grumbler. If we were to stand in front of an imaginary counter top, standing on which are the glasses of the different aspects of our life. Some full to overflowing and some with a bare dribble of water. We have a choice to be grateful for what is there already or to be complaining about what is missing from the glasses.

I was humbled many times listening to some of the children in church, when asked to pray. The simplicity of their prayers and the way they modelled gratitude. Grateful many times, for things many of us have taken for granted, like another year being added to our lives, making it through the previous week safe and well or simply for the gift of another day.

1 Thessalonians 5v18

"Give thanks in all circumstances for this is God's will for you in Christ Jesus"

Colossians 4v2

"Devote yourselves to prayer, being watchful and thankful"

Father, help me today, to spend time focusing and giving thanks for the water already in my glass instead of pining for the empty top half.

The Squabble – Dealing with conflict

Walking past the lake in Farmleigh we heard a commotion. Three coots in close quarters, squawking, flapping their wings at each other, water splashing. They were having a squabble! Out of nowhere a bigger bird, skidded into their midst and put a swift end to the quarrel. The three young coots, took off.

There was no discussion with the adult bird as to who started it, who was right or who in the perceived wrong. Did the parent say "stop" or perhaps "separate"? Two of the young birds restarted the fight on a different part of the lake and again they were swiftly corrected.

When squabbles and bickering start, we could heed the command, (for the way it was given wasn't mere advice) of the adult bird and separate, cool down, stop fighting a point and lay down the desire to be right or victorious in the battle. It takes humility at times to let things go.

Isaiah 32v18

"My people will live in peaceful dwelling places, in secure homes, in undisturbed places of rest"

It's not just in homes and among family members that we could do well at times to end a squabble. Perhaps it's in a church setting, a place of work, with the neighbours, at the school gates, on a sports team or with a group of friends.

Father thank You for Your promise to live in a peaceful dwelling, a secure home and an undisturbed place of rest. Help me to be someone who sows peace and accord. No matter where the setting is, help me to have the wisdom to know when to let things go. May I have the humility to not have to fight, argue or debate a point just for the sake of being right or not wanting to lose face. Please enable me to back down gracefully and be quick to say sorry, forgive and be reconciled.

1 Corinthians 13v5

Love keeps no record of wrongs.

Wounded Heart – **Healing balm**

The recycling went flying through the air into the outside bin, landing with a clatter. Sudden sharp pain in my hand and I hoped the cuts made by the empty tomato tin weren't deep.

I applied pressure, prayed, cleansed and covered the cuts with a plaster. Then returned to what I had previously been doing but even with the small cuts the simple tasks became more arduous. How much more so for one with a deep wound?

We protect a wound from more damage as bangs and knocks can bring further pain or make it weep, bleed or reopen. Dirt can cause it to become infected so we keep the wound clean and dry.

Wounded hearts - some just surface wounds, others deep rivets. They can hold us back and slow us down. They can make us apprehensive of trusting again and cause us to be fearful that the wound will reopen or weep once more. They can stop us from doing what in our hearts we long to do. They can prevent us from following our dreams and pursing our goals.

Psalm 147v3

"He heals the broken hearted and bandages their wounds"

Father I pray for anyone reading this with a hurting, wounded, aching or broken heart. Please heal their broken heart. Help them to trust again and Lord just like we protect physical wounds from becoming infected, help them to protect their hearts from becoming hard or bitter. If the pain was caused by another, help them to forgive the person, people or institution that caused the hurt, be it intentionally or unintentionally. Remove any shame and flood them with Your love that can reach the deepest crevices. In Jesus name I pray.

Isaiah 47v10

"Though the mountains be shaken and the hills be removed, yet my unfailing love for you will not be shaken nor my covenant of peace be removed," says the LORD, who has compassion on you."

Positioning – My place in the kingdom

A lady on the trail in front of me bent down, picked up a long stick, banged it on the ground to test its' strength and passed it to her companion. Now it was a walking stick, offering support.

The birds get busy collecting tiny twigs every Spring to weave into their nests. I pass people in colder seasons, arms laden with small sticks, kindling for their stoves or open fires. Big fallen logs along the path become seats for us to rest and recharge on.

All four are wood, one offered support, one shelter, one warmth and one a place to recharge. A coach or manager knows his team and plays his players where their strengths will be showcased.

Sometimes frustrations can arise simply because people are in places where their strengths are not being used. Some are like the kindling, called to help start and launch a project, ministry or new idea but then once they have got it started the slow burning logs are needed to come and keep the fire burning. The enthusiastic kindling has moved on to help ignite another project. Kindling in an open fire, ignites quickly and burns up quickly. The walking stick would have a hard job fitting into a nest building project and the flimsy twigs don't have the strength or height to become a walking stick.

1 Corinthians 12v5&6

"There are different kinds of service, but the same Lord. There are different kinds of working, but in all of them and in everyone it is the same God at work"

Father help us to appreciate the strengths and gifts that You have given to each of Your children. Help us to recognise while different service it is the same Lord. If there is a repositioning needed in my life, may the move be seamless. Please let each one of us do our part to sow love and harmony in the house of the Lord and let there be no bickering, jealousy or competition among Your children. May we remember that we are playing on the one team, just in different positions.

Easy Pickings – Salvation

The thud of the cracker hitting the shed roof was met by instant caws overhead. This was easy pickings, a free meal. No digging of beaks in rock solid ground for grubs. No tearing apart a discarded paper bag in search of the last soggy chip. This time the cawing crow had to simply receive what had been bought and paid for by somebody else.

John 3v16

"For God so loved the world that he gave his only begotten son that whoever believes in him shall not perish but have everlasting life"

Salvation is a free gift that can't be bought, earned or worked for. An unmerited gift, bought and paid for by another that simply needs to be received.

Ephesians 2v8

"For by grace you have been saved, through faith and that not of yourselves; it is the gift of God"

When someone gets a gift, many times they excitedly tell others about it. Time passes, the newness wears off and they stop talking about the gift. Perhaps for some of us the excited newness of our salvation is a long time ago.

The caws of the solitary crow had alerted his companions who perched on overhead wires, sat on the roof of the house and balanced on thin branches. This was news too good to keep to himself. This was news worth sharing.

Romans 10v14&15

"How, then, can they call on the one they have not believed in? And how can they believe in the one of whom they have not heard? And how can they hear without someone preaching to them? And how can anyone preach unless they are sent? As it is written: "How beautiful are the feet of those who bring good news!"

Father help me today to not keep to myself news that is meant for sharing. Present me with opportunities today and may I have the courage to not let them slip me by. Help me to not make excuses as to why I can't share the good news but rather to follow Your leading and guiding in Jesus' name.

Inaccessible places - Contentment

The child asks you to get them a game, toy or activity that they can't reach. The thing they want is on the very top shelf, buried beneath everything else. In your view inaccessible. You try in vain to persuade them of the merits of the toys already sprawled across the floor.

I was praying about a "top shelf" or "back of the shelf" situation. I felt to stop, and reflect on what I already have in relation to that situation, like a child with a floor full of toys and activities in front of them. There are times we put so much time and energy thinking about the things that are not, that we can overlook what we already have in an area.

Perhaps your top shelf situation is a new home, but where you now live are good neighbours, great public transport, an easy commute, low rent. Maybe it's a job and in the meantime, you could overlook how blessed you are with current colleagues in a nice work environment. Most parents are always praying about one situation or another regarding our children, I don't believe this ever stops. But, do we take time to reflect on what is already there? The stages pass so quickly, if we're not careful, they will pass us by. I took a moment as I prayed about the "top of the shelf" situation and started to give thanks for all the things that were on the lower shelves. The list became longer than I could ever have imagined.

Ephesians 5v20

"Giving thanks always for all things to God the father in the name of our Lord Jesus Christ"

Take a moment if you can, reflect, list off in your head, write or type the things currently sprawled out before you as you trust God for that "top of the shelf" or "back of the shelf" situation. It doesn't mean we don't keep praying, trusting and thanking Him for the inaccessible things but it makes the waiting time more enjoyable and less arduous. I walked many kilometres with my young adult children during the covid-19 pandemic, while I was not thankful for the virus or lockdowns. There are things I was grateful for in that season. I had so many opportunities to spend time with my nearly grown children. They were great company, many miles were covered, we prayed, laughed, talked, attended online services, baked, cooked, watched movies, ate together, washed endless delph and made wonderful memories. So even in the harder times, we can still find things to be grateful for.

Father I choose to be grateful today for what is already on the floor before me, help me not to take these things for granted as I pray about the "top shelf" or "back of the shelf" situations, but rather to embrace what I already have, in Jesus' name I pray.

Have faith in God – Faith

Have faith in God are words I was meditating on recently from Mark 11. We can ask ourselves – where am I putting my faith? In what am I trusting? In whom am I hoping?

Romans 4v18

"Against all hope, Abraham in hope believed"

In the natural there wasn't any hope for Abraham. He knew circumstances were against both him and his wife Sarah. But Abraham had a promise from God and in that he chose to trust.

Romans 4 v19

"Without weakening in his faith, he faced the fact that his body was as good as dead since he was about 100 years old and that Sarah's womb was also dead. Yet he did not waver through unbelief regarding the promise of God but was strengthened in his faith and gave glory to God being fully persuaded that God had power to do what he had promised"

Some of us are facing situations in which circumstances are against us and perhaps like for Abraham and Sarah the clock is ticking loudly. Saying time up or too late. However, we can choose to be like Abraham and not consider the circumstances but rather put our hope and trust in His promises. The next part of verse 18 says, "Against all hope, Abraham in hope believed and so became the father of many nations just as had been said to him, so shall your offspring be." Abraham hoped and trusted, he put his faith in God and he saw the manifestation of Gods promise to him.

Perhaps some of us need to remind ourselves of a promise He has made, we may need to dust the cobwebs off it even. We may need to say Father I am sorry for doubting and sorry for giving up because it seemed like it wasn't coming and was never going to happen. The loved one whose salvation I have prayed for seems even more anti God with each passing year. The family feud that I prayed to be resolved has got even more bitter. The financial situation I trusted for has worsened. The marriage that I prayed for, looks even less healthy. The health situation that I believed for healing in has become more serious. We can consider the circumstances or we can against all hope in hope believe.

Today I choose to hope again, I choose to trust again, I choose to have faith in God again for a situation or multiple scenarios.

Light dispels the darkness – Letting our light shine

As I prayed last night, I heard the words; light dispels the darkness. Staying in the countryside last summer I was amazed at how dark it was. Being so used to street lights, lights from passing vehicles and light shining from the windows of homes around me, the pitch black took me by surprise.

When you walk into a darkened room and turn on the light. Which wins - the light or the darkness?

John 9v5

"Jesus spoke to the people and said I am the light of the world"

As Christians we are called not only to walk in the light but to be the light to those around us.

Matthew 6v16

"In the same way let your light shine before others that they may see your good deeds and glorify your Father in heaven"

Walking the country roads at night last summer, from my cousins' home to our holiday home, the light from our phones dispelled the darkness, not in the whole of Ireland or even the whole county of Wexford but in front of us and around us.

Sometimes we can get bogged down thinking and talking about all the darkness that exists, it can feel overwhelming at times. There are those who wonder, what is the point as the darkness is so great. Yet like the torch on our phones, we can start wherever we are shining our lights into the darkness. Not only where we are physically but wherever our sphere of influence is.

Father help me to shine my light for You today. Please give me opportunities today and don't let me allow those opportunities to slip by. Let me remember that, light dispels the darkness.

Today is the Tomorrow - Worry

Today is the tomorrow we may have worried about yesterday. Wise words spoken at a women's meeting recently. If we were to write our worries down today and look back next week, month or year. How much of what we worried about came to pass in our lives, in the lives of loved ones or in society as a whole?

Matthew 6v34

"Therefore, do not worry about tomorrow, for tomorrow will worry about itself. Each day has enough trouble of its own"

If we were to calculate or even make an estimated guess, what would be the sum total of time invested in worry in recent times? Investments pay dividends. Unfortunately, the dividends that worry brings into our lives are neither pleasant nor desirable and can affect many areas of our life. Stealing our peace, disturbing our sleep and even affecting our physical bodies at times. Excess worrying can make us irritable or edgy and thus take a toll on relationships, it can cause distractions thus making it hard to concentrate on the task at hand.

If we put time invested in worrying on one side of a balance scale and time spent in prayer on the other side, which side would be weightier?

Perhaps you are thinking or shouting as you read this - "easy for you to say, you don't know the problems I am facing, you can't see the maze I am in that I have gone around and around in and still can't seem to find the way out".

That's correct, I don't know what you are up against today but He does and our loving Heavenly Father tells each of us today to not worry in Matthew 6v34.

If worry has become a habit and something we slip into easily, we can even worry about the worry. And the thought of not worrying seems an impossibility. However rather than looking at the mountain of worry, if we were to catch each new worry and turn it into a prayer, soon the mountain would become a hill and then a plain.

Father, please forgive me for the times I have worried. Help me to trust You and to turn my worries into prayers in Jesus' name. Thank you that as I do this Your peace which surpasses all understanding will guard my heart and mind in Christ Jesus.

One Day at a Time? – Taking it day by day

Standing on the corridor of the maternity hospital, talking on the public phone. My mother had six words of wisdom for me, as I thought about caring for my new-born twins and their very active two year old brother at home.

"Take one day at a time". My mother was to leave this world six weeks later, her six words of wisdom becoming even more vital for me.

Psalm 37v23

"The steps of a good man are ordered by the Lord"

If we look too far ahead, we might not begin the journey. If we keep wondering what next month or next year holds, we might not set off. If we consider what lies around the corner, we may crumble. But if we take one day at a time, our burden becomes lighter, our journey both easier and more enjoyable.

Trusting Him for the strength, the wisdom and the resolve to make it through today. Then the same tomorrow and the next day. Suddenly we can look back and see how far we have journeyed. It is 19 years since that phone call with my mother.

Psalm 119v105

"Your word is a lamp to my feet and a light to my path"

The oil lamps to which that verse would have referred provided light around the person carrying it, enabling them to see just in front of them and take the next step. Once taken they could see where to take the next one, and then the next one and so on and so forth.

No matter what we face today - a thesis that needs writing, a doctor's diagnosis, a recent bereavement, blending two families, a financial situation, anxiety about the future, a new business venture, a relationship break up - we can decide to take one day at a time.

Father help me to take one day at a time. Thank you for the grace, strength and courage for today in Jesus' name.

Psalm 37v7

"Be still before the Lord and wait patiently for him"

Loneliness

Many had not met Mr lonely until 2020. Many thought their paths would never cross. Some never gave loneliness a second thought as to them it was simply another term in the dictionary and not something they would ever encounter. Then with lockdowns and restrictions, schools and colleges closed, church services online, extra-curricular activities prohibited, many working from home, some not allowed to work, people advised to stay home, people not allowed to travel. People were kept apart from classmates, friends, team mates, neighbours, family, colleagues, church members. No age was exempt.

Going forward perhaps we will have learnt from it and maybe it will have given us a greater empathy and compassion for those who are dealing with Mr Lonely. Many times, people try to tackle him alone and are often too embarrassed to say that he has showed up in their lives, as though there is some sort of shame attached to him being there.

At different stages and for different reasons people may struggle with loneliness. A mother at home with her much loved new born, perhaps far away from family and learning how to sculpt out a new life and build new support systems. A student living away from family for the first time, a widow or widower adjusting to being single again, a parent facing an empty nest, an emigrant living abroad longing for home, someone isolated due to sickness or injury, a person who finds themselves on their own due to a relationship break up, someone recently bereaved, someone who has been excluded and left out by others.

Hebrews 13v15

"I will never leave you nor forsake you"

I pray for those reading this today who are feeling the icy cold that Mr lonely brings in the door with him. Father may they experience the warmth of Your love. May they feel hope today. You promise to never leave nor forsake us. Please put them on someone's heart who will reach out to them today. If there are any practical steps, they themselves can take please give them the strength and courage to do so. You tell us in Psalm 68 that you set the lonely in families.

I pray for those reading this today whose cup is full. Lord, please open eyes both physically and spiritually to the needs of those around them. Let them reach out and share from their full cup with others.

Let yourself off the hook - **Forgiving myself**

The younger generation wouldn't understand what it means when we say the phone was "off the hook". At times on purpose and sometimes inadvertently, the phones handset was left off the hook, but the result was the same, no caller could get through, connect or talk to you.

We use the phrase "let someone off the hook". Meaning we show mercy and forgive them. Some today need to let someone off the hook. For some this person is harder to forgive than parent, spouse, minister, friend, child, co-worker or neighbour. Someone reading this may need to show mercy and let themself off the hook.

What if Paul never let himself off the hook for his behaviour prior to his conversion towards the Christians? What if Peter could never have moved on and forgiven himself for denying Jesus?

Romans 8v1

"There is therefore no condemnation to them which are in Christ Jesus"

The enemy wants to keep us stuck. Stuck in shame, guilt, remorse or regret over things we did, choices we made or decisions we didn't take.

But God wants to set us free and for some today the first step in the process is to forgive themself. Shame and guilt have meant some are like the phone off the hook, unable to fully engage and connect.

Philippians 3v13

"But this one thing I do, forgetting those things which are behind, and reaching forth unto those things which are before"

Mark 11v25

"And when you stand praying, if you hold anything against anyone, forgive them, so that your Father in heaven may forgive you your sins"

Father I choose today to forgive myself for ...... Release me please from the guilt, shame, remorse and regret in Jesus' name. Help me to forget the things which are behind and instead to reach forth to what is ahead, in Jesus' name I pray. Please put me back on the hook and let me be able to fully connect.

The Generations – **Passing it on**

Recently I asked a friend how her husband had come to the Lord. At the start of his story was a grandmother who took her grandchildren to church. Down the road and around a few corners, her husband as a young adult surrendered his life to the Lord.

Over the years in children's ministry there were children who came to church not with parents but brought by aunts, uncles or grandparents.

God is interested in the generations. Sometimes people can become disheartened if they don't see the generation after them walking with the Lord. But take heart and don't let it stop there. Look over their shoulders and beyond to the grandchildren and the great nieces and great nephews.

Psalm 78v4

"We will not hide them from their descendants. We will tell the next generation the praiseworthy deeds of the Lord, his power and the wonders he has done"

Joel 1v3

"Tell your children about it and let your children tell their children and their children the next generation"

Don't swallow any lies the enemy tries to feed you regarding your descendants. Lift your grandchildren and great nieces and great nephews up before the throne of grace. Soak them in love and seek out opportunities to sow the truth of His word in to their hearts and above all let them see Jesus reflected in you, in your attitudes, deeds and words.

Don't be discouraged if you have yet to see any visible fruit from your labours. The bulbs lie dormant beneath the ground for many months before we see any sign of them above ground. So, don't lose heart. My friends' husband is faithfully serving the Lord and bringing his own children up in the ways of the Lord, and it all began with a grandmother.

Father help me to do my part in telling the next generation about You. If I have yet to see results from seeds already sown, help me not to become disheartened but to keep trusting that the seeds sown will produce fruit.

Timed out - Waiting on answers to prayer

When we take too long idle while online, we become "timed out". We rush to finish and display the knowledge we have, but it's "time up" for the exam. We read the warning message that our zoom call is about to run "out of time". We tear to the departure gate only to be told we are "too late", our boarding gate has closed.

Timed out, time up, too late. A wise minister told us recently in a meeting that the word of God doesn't have a "use by date" or a "best before."

The promises He has spoken to your heart, the things you are trusting Him for and believing for don't have a little stamp on them saying "best before" or "use by" which really translates as – if it doesn't happen by a particular date, or in a set time frame well then it is too late.

Psalm 31v15

"My times are in your hands"

Sometimes the hardest thing is just to do nothing and wait. Isaiah 40v31 is a well-known scripture that says "those who wait on the Lord, shall renew their strength". I always saw it as physical strength as it goes on to talk about walking and running. Sometimes where we need strength is not in our limbs but in our soulish realm. Strength to keep trusting, strength to keep swatting away the nasty, persistent doubt that buzzes around our head like an unwanted fly, strength to keep hoping.

Time itself can at times be the greatest enemy of our hope. The thing that tries to steal our joy and to make us question our faith. But today we chose not to think time up, timed out or too late but rather to think "on its' way".

Galatians 6v9

"Let us not become weary in doing good, for at the proper time we will reap a harvest if we do not give up"

Father thank You that Your promises to me and Your promises to each one of us have no use by or best before date. Thank You that they are yes and amen and as fresh as when You first declared them. Father as I wait upon You, please strengthen me today. In Jesus name I pray.

Abandoned – He will never leave you

In recent months there have been many knocks at the front door from the postman or a courier delivering an order or a gift sent. Yesterday there was no phone call, email nor knock on the front door, my daughter simply stumbled across two packages that had been abandoned on the doorstep. She rescued them from where they lay and brought them indoors.

There are people who have suffered abandonment. Maybe they were abandoned by a spouse, a parent, a church leader, a devoted friend or a relative. Some parents can feel abandoned when grown children relocate a long distance away. There are those who have been abandoned by family, friends or colleagues because of their beliefs. They have been excluded, left out, rejected and isolated.

Others have been crying out to God and yet no answer appears to have come, so they can wonder if God has abandoned them.

Isaiah 49v15&16

"I will not forget you! See I have engraved you on the palms of my hands. Your walls are ever before me"

We can rest assured, even if a loved one has abandoned us physically or emotionally that God will never abandon us. In times where we feel all alone, lonely and wonder does anyone even care He tells us "Do not fear for I am with you", Isaiah 41v10. "Be strong and of good courage, do not fear nor be afraid of them, for the Lord your God, He is the one who goes with you. He will not leave you nor forsake you" Deuteronomy 31v6.

Abandonment hurts, not just like a surface scratch but as a deep wound. However, there is no wound too deep that His healing love cannot reach.

Psalm 147v3

"He heals the broken-hearted and binds up their wounds"

For those who suffered abandonment and are fearful of trusting again, He promises that when we seek Him, He will deliver us from all our fears. He can help us trust again.

Father I pray for those who have suffered abandonment at the hands of another. Help them to forgive. Pour Your healing oil into hurting hearts and help them to trust again. Remove any shame the abandonment caused; in Jesus' name I pray.

Tempted – Temptation

The dog charges after me when I go to our outside bin, hoping something will be dropped enroute. She wasn't tempted by this morning's offerings of a banana peel, mushrooms and a cold tea bag. When I go shopping there isn't a battle to be fought with temptation. It never crosses my mind to stuff articles into my bag, up a sleeve or into a pocket unpaid for. I'm not tempted to steal. "Temptation is the desire to do something especially something wrong or unwise."

However, while I may not be tempted to steal there are at times other temptations that come my way. We all face temptations to do or omit to do something, to say something we shouldn't or to or to say it in a particular way or tone that's not right. We can be tempted to entertain certain thought patterns or to have attitudes that aren't right. And for many of us emotions such as anger, hatred, pride, jealousy or unforgiveness come knocking looking to be let in.

1 Corinthians 10v13

"No temptation has overtaken you except what is common to mankind. And God is faithful; he will not let you be tempted beyond what you can bear. But when you are tempted, he will also provide a way out so that you can endure it."

Thank God He has made a way out for us when we are tempted. We can walk or run away from temptation. We can choose to not allow it in or entertain it. Temptation is merely the desire. We have a choice not to yield to it. If we know our area of weakness we can where possible avoid situations where we'll be tempted. If gossip has been a problem, when the juiciest bit of news comes our way, hide the phone, until the desire to spread it passes! If anger is the issue, walk away before the wick gets lit.

Matthew 26v41

"Watch and pray so that you will not fall into temptation, the spirit is willing but the flesh is weak"

When Jesus was tempted by the devil, he used the word of God. He said "it is written". The word of God is our sword, it is our offensive weapon, when temptation comes for come it will, we have a choice to yield to it or pray for strength to resist and use our sword of the spirit which is the word of God. For it is written.

Father help me to watch and pray so that I won't fall into temptation. When temptation comes may I say "it is written…."

Preparation – Seasons of preparation

When you watch a cookery show or a you tube cooking demonstration everything appears quick, easy and hassle free. Then sometimes when you try and replicate it at home, it takes more time, greater effort and creates a larger volume of mess. That's due to the time and effort invested in the preparations ahead of filming. The peeling, weighing, grating, chopping, coring, shredding was over before the camera started to roll.

There are seasons of preparation in our lives. Many times, we want to run from, avoid or shorten these seasons. But preparation time is never wasted time. Who wants to eat an apple pie with pips or chunks of peel? In the seasons of preparation when it can feel like nothing is happening if we surrender to what He wants to do, He will do a work in us, preparing us for the next season, for what's up ahead.

When we are unprepared and ill prepared many times, what should be a joy feels like a hassle, chore and burden.

Sometimes we have cans, packets or jars of spices sitting unopened in the press or larder for a long time and we wonder what use are they and why do we even have them. Then suddenly the day comes and they are required. We may have skills, talents, gifts that we feel are like the unopened jar of spice but up ahead, down the road, around the corner- that skill, talent and gift may prove to be invaluable.

I heard a testimony recently about a young French speaking lady who had her life mapped out. Then God started to speak to her and directed her to do three things, which were to learn English, study the Bible and learn how to run a business. None of these were necessary for what she was planning for her life. However up ahead and down the road she married an English speaking man, who was a pastor and in addition she now runs a Christian publishing company. She didn't know what was down the line, but God did.

Father help us to never shun, run from or try to shorten the seasons of preparation in our lives.

Passing through or planted? – Church

I attempt to prolong the visiting time of flowers in my vase on the window sill by feeding them, changing their water and pulling off dead foliage. But while this extends their visit, there comes a time when they end up in the compost bin. They have stems but no root system.

On the other side of the window pane are flowers in window boxes and bushes and trees in the flower bed. These are not visitors simply passing through but have been planted in my garden. Their roots go down into the soil absorbing water and nutrients, anchoring them, providing support. Their presence in the garden not only blesses me, but those who pass by on the road get to share in their beauty.

Some people are like the flowers in my vase, passing through churches but never putting down roots. There are others though who are like the trees in my garden, who are planted in the House of the Lord. They absorb the word; their root systems provide support no matter what season they are in. Those who are planted produce fruit and are a blessing to others.

Psalm 92v12-15

"The righteous shall flourish like a palm tree. He shall grow like a cedar in Lebanon. Those who are planted in the house of the Lord shall flourish in the courts of our God. They shall still bear fruit in old age; they shall be fresh and flourishing, to declare that the Lord is upright; he is my rock."

Father if I am not planted in the house of the Lord, please plant me. Plant me somewhere where I can put down roots, grow and flourish and become a blessing to others.

How's the cake? - Motivational gifts

The question I asked my husband as he sampled the new recipe. His response was "there isn't much of a lemon taste off it." To taste of lemon drizzle would have been a hard feat for this cake to pull off given that it was an orange cake. It was never intended to be a lemon cake and didn't have the necessary ingredients in it to be a lemon cake. While oranges and lemons belong to the same citrus family, they have different tastes and meet different needs. Not many would fancy a large glass of lemon juice with their breakfast nor a wedge of orange on their salmon.

Romans 12v4-8

"For just as each of us has one body with many members, and these members do not all have the same function, so in Christ we, though many, form one body, and each member belongs to all the others. We have different gifts, according to the grace given to each of us. If your gift is prophesying, then prophesy in accordance with your faith; if it is serving, then serve; if it is teaching, then teach; if it is to encourage, then give encouragement; if it is giving, then give generously; if it is to lead, do it diligently; if it is to show mercy, do it cheerfully"

The seven gifts spoken of in Romans 12 are the motivational gifts, given to equip the believers, when flowing in our area of gifting there is joy and fulfilment. However, when we're an orange trying to fulfil the lemons' role, we can end up feeling frustrated, unfulfilled, disillusioned and may even quit. It can lead to feelings of insecurity, inadequacy and lack of self-worth as we struggle to do something we're not gifted to do.

Mrs Mercy doesn't notice the hours tick by as she sits by a hospital bed, Mr teacher can spend hours by himself studying and preparing a teaching, Mrs administrator gets great fulfilment from organising and the one with the motivational gift to serve has been described as the hands of the body. However how would each of these feel if asked to swap roles with someone else? How effective would they be? No matter what our motivational gifts are, we're all called to serve in the same manner.

Colossians 3v17

"And whatever you do, whether in word or deed, do it all in the name of the Lord Jesus, giving thanks to God the Father through him"

Father for those who have yet to discover their area of gifting please lead and guide them and open the right doors of opportunity to use their gifts to be a blessing to others. Remembering we are never too young to start using our gift or too old to continue using it.

Consistency – **Being consistent**

I heard the Lord say "consistency" last night. It is defined as "the quality of always performing or behaving in a particular way".

Painters will ensure they apply the paint evenly on the wall. Bakers when icing a cake, keep the consistency the same and when making a pie we keep the depth standard throughout the dish or one end risks being raw and the other burnt. Perhaps we could benefit from doing an inventory of self and asking. Am I consistent in my life or would I benefit from greater consistency in certain areas?

Do I let the children climb the curtains one day but make them sit like statues the next? Do I do an all-nighter, stay up and pray fervently and then forget to communicate with heaven for a week? Do I read a book of the Bible one day but a month later I am brushing the dust of my Bible? Do I feast and then fast? Am I high on faith one day and down in the dumps of doubt the next?

There are blessings from being consistent and for some personality types, consistency comes easier than for others.

1 Corinthians 15v58

"Therefore, my beloved brothers, be steadfast, immovable, always abounding in the work of the Lord, knowing that in the Lord your labour is not in vain"

Hebrews 13v8 tells us Jesus is the same yesterday, today and forever.

Father, please shine the spotlight today on any areas of my life that are lacking in consistency. Help me to be steadfast. Give me the grace to change what needs changing. Thank You, Father.

Leap of faith - Faith

We walked and picnicked often by the river in Powerscourt Estate when our children were young. If we wandered off the path, under the trees by the river bank, there was great delight when a homemade swing was found. Hanging enticingly from a tall branch overhead, the rope dangled out of reach above the icy water. If you fancied a turn on the swing you had to do a running leap from the bank, jump out over the water, arms outstretched, hoping you caught the swing and didn't end up taking a bath in river water.

Hebrews 11v1

"Now faith is the substance of things hoped for the evidence of things not seen"

Most of us are trusting God for something, most are praying about situations, many of us have faith for things which have yet to manifest in the natural realm. But when we come out of our prayer closet and when we leave the prayer meeting do our words line up with how we have prayed and do our actions show what we are believing in our heart?

Perhaps it's time to take a running leap of faith. Charge down the embankment, arms outreached towards Him, fully believing and trusting Him to catch us when we jump and not let us fall. The voice of logic will try and drown out our faith at times, the voice of reason will scream above it. What we are seeing, hearing and experiencing will try and quash it and keep us from taking that leap.

Some reading this may be like the person who wanted to have a swing but wanted the security of the bank and tried to keep one foot firmly on the bank. So, they never left the river bank. He is calling us to a walk of faith and not a hop of faith.

James 2v14

"What good is it, dear brothers and sisters, if you say you have faith but don't show it by your actions?"

Father help me to take that leap of faith, it is faith and not folly when I am trusting in You. Help me to have the faith to leave the security of the bank behind me, in Jesus' name I pray.

43

Blow out - **When we blow it**

Perhaps driving the dual carriageway or motorway, you have spotted pieces of tyre strewn along the road. A motorist who has driven the road ahead of you had a blowout. When a tyre blows out it is beyond repair. It can't be mended, fixed or patched up. Have you ever thought or said "well I have blown it" or been told by another "you have really blown it this time?" With that thought or those words can come the feeling that, there's no hope similar to the unrepairable tyre after the blow out. The words of a song jumped out at me the other day as I listened – "we go from glory to glory to glory, never be the same." Good words to be reminded of when we feel like we have "blown it" in an area or multiple areas of our life.

2 Corinthians 3v18

"But we all, with unveiled face, beholding as in a mirror the glory of the Lord, are being transformed into the same image from glory to glory, just as by the Spirit of the Lord"

Another version says "the Lord - who is the Spirit-makes us more and more like him as we are changed into his glorious image." We are being changed or transformed into His image; it's a process that takes time. When we do "blow it", Ephesians 2 tells us that God is rich in mercy. Mercy being "compassion or forgiveness shown towards someone whom it is within one's power to punish or harm". Rich in mercy, not stingy and withholding of mercy and it doesn't have to be begged for or extracted from His hand like someone unwilling to hand over something. Gods' mercy means that He doesn't punish us like we deserve for our sin.

1 John 1v9

"If we confess our sins, he is faithful and righteous to forgive us our sins and to cleanse us from all unrighteousness"

Lamentations 3v22&23

"The steadfast love of the Lord never ceases, his mercies never come to an end; they are new every morning; great is your faithfulness"

Even if we blew it yesterday, His reserve of mercy was not depleted. The verse in Lamentations says his mercies never come to an end; they are new every morning.

Father thank You for reminding me that we are being changed from glory to glory into your image. Thank You that Your mercies are new every day and You are always ready and willing to forgive me and never say, "not again!"

Pancakes – Trials

Often on a Sunday evening growing up, sitting around the fire we would eat drop scones. These in effect being more of a mini pancake than a scone and a perfect alternative for those who struggled to flip a pancake. Pouring the liquid batter onto the pan for my own children the other night, I watched it take shape when it hit the heat of the frying pan. Which of us would volunteer to endure the heat of a trial? Who wants to go through a fiery situation? None of us, but just like the heat of the frying pan moulded the batter and shaped my dropped scones so too can the trials that we walk through as Christians help shape us.

James 1v2-4

"My brethren, count it all joy when you fall into various trials, knowing that the testing of your faith produces patience. But let patience have its perfect work, that you may be perfect and complete, lacking nothing"

The soft batter gradually hardened in the heat. Pain, loss, suffering, hardship, disappointment and tragedy though not things we want, choose or wish for can in fact strengthen us. "Hardships often prepare ordinary people for an extraordinary destiny." C.S. Lewis

Sometimes we meet someone on our journey through life who has a depth of characteur. Oft times that has come from digging down and digging deep when things were hard and difficult. From not jumping ship when adversity came but picking up a bucket and emptying the water that crashed in over the sides thus preventing their vessel from sinking. When we walk through a trial and make it to the other side, often times we have greater humility, greater trust in Him and greater empathy for others and what they are walking through.

2 Corinthians 1v4

"Who comforts us in all our troubles, so that we can comfort those in any trouble with the comfort we ourselves receive from God"

If you find yourself in the midst of a fiery trial today or multiple trials you can take heart knowing that He has promised in Psalm 34v19 to deliver you out of every one.

Father strengthen me as I walk through this trial and do a work in me.

Gods Medicine

When people think of 1940, they probably think of World War two. When we think of 2001, we most likely will remember that is the year of the 9/11 tragedy. In years to come when people remember and talk of 2020 it will no doubt be remembered for covid-19. It won't be remembered for war, acts of terrorism but for sickness.

Proverbs 4v20-22

"My son, give attention to my words; incline your ear to my sayings. Do not let them depart from your eyes; keep them in the midst of your heart; for they are life to those who find them, and health to all their flesh"

Proverbs 4 v 20 says to give attention to His word or other versions say to "attend to His word". It says "incline your ear to my sayings". When we incline to hear something, we listen actively, we put ourselves in a position to hear. We are told to keep His word in the midst of our heart and not to let His words depart from our eyes. The reason being to give attention, incline our ears, keep in our heart and eyes is that these words are life to those who find them and health to their flesh.

This medication is freely available to all, no doctors visit is required, no diagnosis necessary. You don't need a prescription to be able to avail of it. It doesn't come with an instruction leaflet which includes possible adverse side effects from taking it. It will never run out. You won't have to drive around looking for a 24/7 pharmacy to buy it. You don't have to watch the clock and calculate if sufficient hours have passed since your last dose to make it safe to take the next dose. You can't take too much of it. You don't need to be sick, in pain or have symptoms to take His medicine. It can be taken at any time, in any season and anywhere.

Thank God for His medicine today. Help me to be diligent to take it.

Courage is Contagious – Take courage

Have you ever thrown a stick in a river and watched it move upstream against the current? The stick or the homemade boat with its leaf sail will flow downstream carried along by the current. If there's a large crowd of people moving in the one direction, it's easy to join the crowd and move along with them in the same direction. It takes agility to move against a flowing crowd.

I was preparing something on wisdom and heard the word fortitude so changed direction. Fortitude being the strength of characteur that enables a person to endure pain or adversity with courage.

Isaiah 53v7

"He was oppressed and he was afflicted, yet he opened not his mouth, like a lamb that is led to the slaughter and like a sheep before its shearers is silent so he opened not his mouth"

It's easy to go with the crowd and hold commonly held beliefs or socially acceptable beliefs. However, as Christians we are called to be followers of Christ and not of the crowd.

Matthew 4v19

"Jesus said "come follow me"

Billy Graham is quoted as saying "courage is contagious. When a brave man takes a stand, the spines of others are stiffened." Many times, we think of bravery as someone who is involved in an extreme sport or walks a tightrope or jumps from a parachute. However, oftentimes being brave and courageous is simply holding onto your biblically held belief in the face of ridicule, judgement, contempt or mockery. Not simply holding onto a belief but living accordingly and refusing to bow under pressure. For some it means being shunned and ostracised by family or friends. Left out.

Father help me to be brave today. Help me to be courageous. Help me to fear not their faces, though many times now it is not faces but words on a screen. Thank You for Your boldness today.

Deuteronomy 31v6

"Be strong and of good courage, do not fear nor be afraid of them; for the LORD your God, He is the One who goes with you. He will not leave you nor forsake you."

Treading water – **Don't panic**

Anyone who learnt to swim would have been taught to tread water. Treading water is the ability to keep your head above water while swimming upright or staying in the one place. It's an essential skill to have for water safety. If in difficulty we can tread water until help arrives. Another skill we were taught is how to float, we were told that if in trouble in the water, to not panic, stay calm and float until help arrived.

We learnt to wave our arm to attract the attention of someone on the shoreline or to blow the whistle if wearing a life jacket. Those in boats and vessels send up distress flares. Perhaps those in a sea of difficulties today or facing a river of problems can apply the swimming advice we learnt.

Stay calm and don't panic. Tread water and don't waste unnecessary energy doing things which aren't helping the situation. If it's something that you can't deal with yourself. Shout for help, wave your arm or blow the whistle. At times we need to do something to attract the attention of another to make them aware of our situation. Sometimes we are waiting for someone to reach out to us and can even get upset at others when no help is forthcoming. Perhaps we need to send up the distress flare to alert others of our need for help.

If we are on dry land walking the river bank or strolling the shoreline, we need to be in tune, watching out for those in difficulty. Looking out for the waving arm on the horizon. Listening for the sound of a whistle on the water. We can be proactive and look into the distance with the binoculars.

Galatians 6v2

"Bear one another's burdens, and so fulfil the law of Christ"

A different version says to carry one another's burdens or another version says share one another's burdens. How much lighter is a burden if carried by another? Sharing a problem or difficulty with someone not only lightens our load but opens the door for prayer and practical supports.

Proverbs 3v27

"Do not withhold good from those to whom it is due, when it is in your power to act"

Father for those in difficulty today, please give strength and courage to send up the distress signal and the ability to stay calm until help arrives. If the shoe is on the other foot, help us to be in tune to the needs of those around us who need help, even if they aren't waving a distress flag. Please help us to be sensitive to the promptings of the still small voice within as You lead and guide us who to pray for and who to reach out to in love and on a practical level.

Blinkers on - **Staying focused**

Many of us probably have childhood memories of skipping. Not skipping a meal or school but skipping for entertainment with a rope. Group skipping was the most fun, a long thick rope twirled between the hands of two children while a third, watched the rope intently. They carefully picked their moment and ran into the middle and started jumping. The trick for the skipper was to keep their eyes on the rope. If they got distracted or misjudged the timing, they got entangled in the rope.

Blinkers are worn often by working horses on their eyes. Horses have great peripheral vision but blinkers prevent them looking sideways or backwards, forcing them to look forward. Concentrating solely on the path ahead of them. Blinkers stop them going backwards, wandering in the wrong direction or getting spooked by something they see or hear around them.

There are times we could all benefit from some blinkers. To keep our focus on the road ahead of us, to prevent us from wandering backwards or sideways or getting spooked by things we see around us.

Jeremiah 29v11 is a very well-known and often quoted scripture. "For I know the plans I have for you," declares the LORD, "plans to prosper you and not to harm you, plans to give you hope and a future"

Different versions word it differently. He has plans to prosper you, He has good plans for you, plans for your welfare, plans for your well-being. He has a good plan for each of us and we need to put on the blinkers, not be spooked by what we are reading or seeing, not be tempted to go off course but keep our focus on the truth from Jeremiah 29v11 – He has a good plan for me, He doesn't have a plan to cause me harm, He has plans to give me both hope and a future.

Psalm 138v8

"The Lord will fulfil His purpose for me"

Father help me today to stay focused, help me to not be spooked by things around me but to keep my eyes and ears on Your promise from Jeremiah, that You have a plan for me. Thank You that You will fulfil your purpose for me.

Ease of passage – Hard times

Growing up we had a wide staircase with a shiny banister that finished in a loop at the bottom. I never counted the stairs but there were four flights. For ease of passage some chose to climb onto the banister and slide down, hopeful not to be caught in the act. Others would attempt to see how many they could jump at a go for this made the journey shorter and for the more adventurous sliding down the stairs inside a sleeping bag made for something different if you were willing to endure the bumps. Most of the time though we had to walk down, a step at a time.

How many of us today would like an easier journey? Who would like to be able to slide to the bottom of a situation? Who would choose to avoid certain things by jumping over them? Often times we pray and ask God for ways out of situations and sometimes rather than giving us a banister He enables and helps us to walk each step, one at a time.

Isaiah 43v2

"When you go through deep waters, I will be with you. When you go through rivers of difficulty, you will not drown. When you walk through the fire of oppression, you will not be burned up; the flames will not consume you"

He promises to be with us in the deep waters, He prevents us from drowning in rivers of difficulty and stops us being burnt by the fires of oppression.

Deuteronomy 31v6

"Be strong and courageous. Do not be afraid or terrified because of them, for the LORD your God goes with you; he will never leave you nor forsake you."

Perhaps you have been putting off a gp visit out of fear of the diagnosis or have avoided confronting a difficult situation out of fear of the reaction. Maybe you have turned a blind eye to things that need dealing with, hoping they will disappear in a puff of smoke. Maybe there is a staircase of debt before you and you have been ignoring the warning letters.

Whatever the staircase looks like before us, no matter how steep or how many steps, we can have peace in our hearts knowing that He will help us down, we just need to put our foot on the top step and start the descent.

Father, please help me today if I am standing looking at a staircase that I have avoided out of fear or for some other reason. Please give me an assurance in my heart that You are with me and You will lead, help and guide me. Thank You, Father, for never leaving nor forsaking me.

Second chances – God's mercy

We stayed in a property where not only the floor boards were reclaimed pitch pine but the kitchen presses too. This timber had been pulled out of old buildings and rather than seeing the end of its days and being thrown in a skip. It had been given a second chance. Each board seeped in history, had its' own story but had been given a fresh start. How many times in frustrations are the words spoken – "you have blown all your chances", "you're on your last chance" or "no more chances?" In different scenarios, words spoken often times in exasperation by a parent, teacher, guardian, boss, coach, minder, youth worker or spouse. Thank God we have a heavenly Father who never says "you have blown your last chance" like the final little candle on a cake to be extinguished. None of us desires to live life on the edge but thank God He is the God of the second chance and the third and the thirty third when we need it.

Lamentations 3v22-23

"The steadfast love of the Lord never ceases, his mercies never come to an end, they are new every morning; great is your faithfulness"

No matter how many times, no matter how far, His mercies have not ended and will not end. Mercy means "compassion or forgiveness shown towards someone whom it is within one's power to punish or harm." Perhaps it is not a case of needing the mercy of God for an area of habitual sin but maybe we have been like Jonah and have run from what we know He has asked us to do. There are many reasons or excuses made for not obeying and running from our calling. Jonah was given a second chance and that time he obeyed. We too with humble hearts can ask for a second chance or opportunity.

Jonah 3v1

"Then the word of the Lord came to Jonah a second time"

People can be hard on us and remind us of our fallings and failings, the enemy can use a mega phone to shout at us and we ourselves can sometimes be the one who is doing the most shouting. Thank God for a heavenly Father who we can run to and not from like the prodigal son to his father. He is waiting with opened arms, arms full of compassion for He is longsuffering and abundant in mercy.

Psalm 86v15

"But you, O Lord are a God full of compassion, and gracious, longsuffering and abundant in mercy and truth"

Father thank You for your mercy today. Thank You that you are the God of the second chance.

Cultivating Friendships - **Friendship**

Sitting recently in the company of friends I thought - families we are born into but our friends we chose. The word friendship conjures up many images for me - love, laughter, encouragement, companionship, shared interests, listening ear, conversation, problems shared, wisdom imparted, celebrations, comfort and more. Stored in the vaults of my heart are many treasured memories of friends and friendships.

Proverbs 27v9

"Ointment and perfume delight the heart and the sweetness of a man's friend gives delight by hearty counsel"

My eyes were drawn to words on a blanket as I hoovered this morning - "it takes a long time to grow an old friend". When you walk past or visit a beautiful mature garden, you can be sure that countless hours were spent getting the garden to look like that and then further hours to keep it looking that way. Unfortunately, good and lasting friendships don't just happen, they don't grow by themselves. They, like the show piece garden require an investment of time and commitment. Then periodically raking, pulling up of weeds and cutting back overgrown briars are necessary to keep the friendship healthy.

Proverbs 17v9

"Love prospers when a fault is forgiven but dwelling on it separates close friends"

Today let's take a few minutes to appreciate our friends, some, a part of our lives for a long time, while others are recent additions. Friends who have left this world before us, but their memory is alive in our hearts. At times people have looked out at a garden that has been neglected and overlooked and wondered where to start. Help us Father to make time for the friendships that we have neglected and overlooked. Those that have been damaged by the action of one or both parties, please let the healing process begin today. Please give us wisdom how to repair, strengthen and fix what has become broken or strained.

Father thank You today for the wonderful gift of friendship! Thank You for my friends, help me not to take any for granted. Enable and equip me to be a good friend. In Jesus name I pray.

Proverbs 18v24

"There is a friend who sticks closer than a brother"

Clouds overhead – **Our refuge**

Has anyone ever said or thought; I can't enjoy life "with this hanging over me" or "when a situation is resolved or gone then I'll be able to fully embrace life again?" It reminds me of trying to enjoy the sun in Ireland, plastering on factor 50 and lying on the sun lounger, or setting the table for the outdoor meal or sprawling on a blanket with a book that has to be finished. Just when everything looks perfect and feels good, an ominous, dark cloud rolls in overhead. An abiding childhood memory with a mother who loved the sea, is shivering in a towel, looking upward to see where the sun had gone, enquiring when it was going to make a reappearance.

The sun had gone nowhere, it was just temporarily blocked from vision by the clouds. If we were to leave the beach every time a cloud appeared, our visits would have been short. Many times, we had just warmed up after the first cloud had blown over, when a second would appear. There's a parallel in our lives, not with physical clouds, but with problems, difficulties, issues, trials and tribulations.

Psalm 34v19

"Many are the afflictions of the righteous"

Often times we have just recovered from the chill of a first affliction when a different one appears. The later part of the verse says – But the Lord delivers him out of them all. It can be a decision to enjoy the beach or the meal outside even when clouds hang threateningly above. So too in the midst of an affliction it's a decision to keep trusting Him, to keep praying, to sing praises and to keep embracing and enjoying life. When we don't feel like praying and singing praises doesn't make sense, that's when we do it in faith and as an act of obedience.

Psalm 59v25

"But I will sing of your strength, in the morning I will sing of your love; for you are my fortress, my refuge in times of trouble"

I'm sure at times we can all relate to the two first words of the verse – "But I". When circumstances ask us is there anything to sing about, we make a choice to sing. When we have sung the last note, the cloud may still be looming overhead, the sky may even have darkened but hopefully our mood will have lifted and we will have found comfort knowing that He is our fortress, our refuge in time of trouble and has promised to deliver us out of every cloudy affliction.

Father help me to look beyond any clouds today. Help me to trust You in spite of any affliction that I may be facing today. Thank You for Your peace today.

Time up - Procrastination

The baking timer rests on the kitchen counter, ticking, counting down until a bell rings. Some probably remember the sensation of sitting in an exam hall, scribbling fast, brain working quicker than pen can write, still so much more knowledge to showcase before the words are uttered, "time up, pens down." It's amazing what can be achieved and accomplished when we have a limited time frame to do it in. The pressure of the ticking clock makes us act and act fast. I learnt about procrastination in leaving cert English when I met Hamlet the procrastinator. The definition of procrastination is "delaying or postponing something". I thought the synonyms written under the definition help explain it further – dithering, stalling, dilly dallying, humming and hawing.

I am sure we can all relate and say we have stalled at times to make a decision; we have dithered about making an apology, we have dilly dallied about doing what we know we should do, we have hummed and hawed about dealing with a work, home, church or friendship issue, we have put on the long finger certain things we don't like or enjoy doing. At times the baking timer goes off, the baker resets it as decides the cake or bread needs more oven time. Some of us have reset timers again and again. If the baker keeps resetting the clock, eventually they will end up with a tin of embers. And unfortunately, it is too late after an exam script has been handed up to add to it the thing you remembered on the way out of the exam hall.

Perhaps today is the day to do some of the things we've been putting off. While some people find this hard to understand, making decisions can be difficult for others. We can choose to show compassion and restraint when we find it frustrating that someone won't decide. Rather than judging, complaining to them or about them we can choose to be understanding. We can turn our exasperation at them to prayers for them and also offer practical advice if they are open to receiving it.

2 Corinthians 12v9

"My grace is sufficient for you, for my power is made perfect in weakness"

Isaiah 30v21

"Whether you turn to the right or to the left, your ears will hear a voice behind you saying, "this is the way, walk in it.""

Father, please help me to not procrastinate. Help me in this season to do the things I need to do; deal with the things which need dealing with and make the decisions I need to make. If I don't struggle in this area but am close to someone who does, please help me to be patient, empathetic and understanding with the individual.

Take shelter - Shielded from harm

Walking and getting caught out by an unexpected downpour, we can choose to walk on until soaked through or we can choose to find shelter until the clouds have blown over. Scorching heat, we can sit, lye, walk or work in it or decide to find shade until it cools down. A small boat pulls inside the harbour wall when caught off guard by a storm to takes refuge from strong winds and high seas. The light aircraft shelters on the ground until the electric storm has passed before taking off. To shelter means to "protect or shield from something harmful"

Psalm 91v1&2

"Whoever dwells in the shelter of the Most High will rest in the shadow of the almighty, I will say of the Lord, He is my refuge and my fortress, my God, in Him I will trust"

How many times have we required shelter? To be sheltered from a physical danger or situation. To be protected from the effects of a fiery trial or from gale force anger. To take refuge from icy atmospheres that make work or home life unpleasant. Who has needed a fortress from false allegations and accusations that blew against you? Perhaps shelter is required from a downpour of hurtful words. Nowadays, keyboard warriors can type harsh, untrue, judgemental and hateful things. At times refuge is required from crashing waves of isolation, rejection and exclusion.

When the heavy rain stopped the walker left their place of shelter dry, when the sun went down the person who had sheltered left that place, not painfully burnt. The little boat left the harbour still intact when the storm ceased and waves had subsided. When the thunder and lightning had passed the light aircraft was unaffected as it had sheltered in the hangar.

Ecclesiastes 7v12

"Wisdom is a shelter"

Sometimes knowing what to do in a difficult situation can be the shelter that we need. Having the wisdom what to do can be the shelter we need from the anguish in our soul. James 1v5 says that if we lack wisdom, we should ask God, who gives "liberally to all" or "generously to all."

Psalm 46v10

"God is our refuge and strength, a very present help in trouble"

Thank You, Father, for being my shelter, my place of refuge, One, who never sleeps or slumbers but is my 24/7 security.

Still producing fruit – Wisdom which comes with age

In one of the local parks where I walk cordoned off is a beautiful, large old tree. Stuck to a timber post beside it, is the tree's story and reason that it now has to be felled. At times we read or hear of people fighting to prevent old trees from being removed to make way for bus lanes or road widening projects. Sometimes there is a carrot dangled of new saplings being planted in their place. A row of freshly planted saplings can't always offer the same appeal as trees that have stood for many years, sometimes hundreds of years. The value of older trees is recognised. An old tree is beautiful to behold, has wide trunks to climb, the spread of its foliage capable of providing shelter from sun and rain.

Proverbs 20v29 amplified

"The glory of young men is their [physical] strength, and the honour of aged men is their grey head [representing wisdom and experience]."

Nonfiction sections of libraries or book shops are full of books written by people who have already climbed the mountain you are considering climbing, visited the city you're booked to visit, set up a business similar to the one you are in the process of starting, raised their children etc. It can make our journey easier when we learn from someone who has already taken a similar journey. We read their books to glean from their wisdom and experience. Isn't it better to hear from another that there is a pothole around the bend than to drive into ourselves and ruin our tyre? So too in the journey of life, we can learn from someone who is further up the road than us.

Job 12v12

"Is not wisdom found among the aged? Does not long-life bring understanding?"

Psalm 92v12-15

"The righteous shall flourish like a palm tree, he shall grow like a cedar in Lebanon. Those who are planted in the house of the Lord shall flourish in the courts of our God. They shall still bear fruit in old age; they shall be fresh and flourishing, to declare that the Lord is upright; He is my rock, and there is no unrighteousness in Him."

Father God I pray that the younger people will seek out and draw from the well of wisdom and experience of the older people in their lives. I pray that the older people will be willing to draw up their buckets and share from their wisdom and experience.

Pulled the short straw – Rejoicing with others

On two occasions recently, I have gone for a coffee with my hubby. Both times mine came served in nice large cups and while I was still sipping, his were long gone for his came in tiny cups. This was not as he expected when he ordered. We could say "he pulled the short straw". The method we used sometimes as children to determine who got to sit in the third row in the estate car, the camp bed on holiday or had last pick off the list of household jobs.

Now my husband could be envious of the extra millilitres of coffee in my cups or he could be glad for me. Romans 12v15 tells us to rejoice with those who rejoice. Rejoice means to feel or show great joy or delight. If we are honest, at times when we are left holding the short straw it can be hard to show great joy or delight for the person who in effect may have what we would like to have.

It can be an act of obedience at times to "rejoice with those who rejoice" when we have prayed and are in the waiting room for what they received or what has happened for them. To be invited to another hen party, when longing to be the one hosting the hen party, it can be a choice to rejoice with the bride to be. When a family member shares the good news that they are expecting their third child, while you are still waiting for a first positive pregnancy test. It can be a decision to rejoice.

While struggling with a child who has gone off the rails who you are storming heaven for, and your best friends' children seem to never put a foot out of place and have one achievement after the next. It can be a decision to rejoice with that friend and not to ignore their calls for you don't want to hear any more about their seemingly perfect offspring.

Your cousin gets a beautiful new house and you have moved so many times, that you don't even bother to unpack the boxes any more. It is a choice to rejoice with your cousin. You have studied hard and earned many qualifications and then your co-worker who is less qualified gets a promotion, you are faced with a choice.

Then you hear the whisper from God – buy the co-worker a congratulations card and a box of chocolates, or give your cousin the beautiful table that you bought in faith for the day you own your first home or offer to mind your family members older children so they can spend quality time with their new arrival.

Sometimes it is doubly hard to rejoice with another when we have waited much longer or things seem to have come to them much easier. The road to answered prayer for us has may have had many pot holes of delays and been twisty. So, at times we feel like we are never going to get to the desired destination whether it be - saying I do, welcoming a new baby,

Pulled the short straw – **Rejoicing with others**

turning the key in the lock of a new home, seeing the prodigal in the distance making their way home, getting the overdue promotion, hearing the words "all clear" and on and on we could go. But in the meantime, as we journey down the road, we can make the decision, to "rejoice with those who rejoice".

Father help me to "rejoice with those who rejoice" even when at times and for different reasons it can be hard. Please reveal to me if I have let envy or jealousy into my heart, so I can repent and pull out any envy seeds. Show me how I can practically demonstrate to those around me that I am rejoicing with them.

Heritage from the Lord - **Children are a blessing**

Psalm 127V3-5

"Children are a heritage from the Lord. The fruit of the womb is a reward. Like arrows in the hand of a warrior. So are the children of one's youth. Happy is the man who has his quiver full of them. They shall not be ashamed"

God says our children are a reward or another version says a gift. It may not always feel like that - when you have a baby that doesn't sleep, a toddler who throws tantrums, a cheeky or awkward child, a sullen teenager, a rebellious, wayward child or a young adult intent on going what appears to be the wrong way and who won't listen to advise. No matter how it feels or looks, God says, children are a reward. Not a burden, something bothersome, a great expense, or an interruption to our life plans.

I heard a preacher say recently, that words spoken once about her as a child, which she overheard, replayed many times in the chambers of her mind. The echo of those words was not music to her ears. Words can define a child. We need to be careful what we say to our children and about them in their hearing. What seeds are we sowing into their hearts? Are they seeds that say they are a blessing, loved, wanted, favoured?

There is a time and place to correct and discipline the behaviours and attitudes of our children but harsh words spoken in anger or rage about the character of a child can be very damaging. If we don't like the way the arrow is heading, sometimes we need to take the focus off the arrow and start looking at the warrior who is responsible for directing these arrows and keeping them on target.

Father help us see our children as rewards and gifts from You. Forgive us for the times we've spoken to them in anger; help us to have the humility to admit to our children when we're wrong. Please give us wisdom how to direct these arrows. If we were on the receiving end of harsh words from a parent, guardian or step parent, please help us to forgive, even if many years have passed since those words were spoken and even if the person has since died.

Not a dress rehearsal -The real thing

Before any live performance opens to the public there are plenty of rehearsals. Lots of practises in empty halls or theatres. No applause, laughter, shrieks of delight or critiques from the audience. Then comes the dress rehearsal, where the cast don their costumes and run through as if it's the "real thing". Notes are made of last minute improvements that can be made for the "real thing."

There's a show on television, prize stakes are high and participants have the option of one "trial run" before they decide whether they will attempt a challenge and risk losing the prize money they've already won.

In life we don't get to do a "trial run" nor do we have a "dress rehearsal". Each day lived is an actual performance. If yesterday had been a "trial run" or if last week was a "dress rehearsal" what would we have done differently? We could ask the same about last month, year or even the last decade.

Each new day is a gift to be embraced and lived to the full. Sometimes it can feel like we are waiting for the curtains to pull back and for the show to begin, rather than embracing each day with excitement and expectancy.

I read a testimony recently of somebody who wanted to do the extraordinary for God. Many of us can relate to that, wanting to do the big things and maybe even saying no to some "ordinary" requests because we are waiting on "extraordinary" to make an appearance. The woman got a call, she had impacted someone's life in her classroom and they were ringing to tell her about it. A life turned around, a young man who became a Christian the year she taught him and so too his family and he was studying to become a youth minister. We can't let ordinary slip past by being too preoccupied searching for extraordinary.

Psalm 118v24

"This is the day that the Lord has made. We will rejoice and be glad in it"

Father help me to remember that life is not a dress rehearsal for the real show. Help me to embrace and be thankful for each new day and the opportunities it brings. Help me to embrace the "ordinary" and look for opportunities to do good, show love and be a witness and not miss them while in a frantic search for "extraordinary".

Pity Vs Compassion

In your hour of need which would you rather meet, someone who will look at you with pity in their eyes or one who will extend the hand of compassion? In many instances, pity will notice the plight of others, pity may talk about it, photograph it or video it. But when pity moves on has the plight of the one, they were looking at changed in any way? Compassion when faced with the same scenario, reaches out to help, to soothe, to listen, to offer prayer, to give comfort. Compassion offers to bear another's burdens for a burden shared is much easier and lighter to carry, than when carried alone. The greatest act of compassion was Jesus going to the cross for me, for you, for mankind. When He walked this earth, He had compassion on the people and He acted out of this compassion.

Matthew 14v13 &14

"When Jesus heard what had happened, he withdrew by boat privately to a solitary place. Hearing of this, the crowds followed him on foot from the towns. When Jesus landed and saw a large crowd, he had compassion on them and healed their sick"

Further on in this chapter we read how the disciples wanted to send the crowds away as it was late and they were in a remote place but instead Jesus fed them. He took care of their physical needs.

2 Corinthians 1v3&4

"Praise be to the God and Father of our Lord Jesus Christ, the Father of compassion and the God of all comfort, who comforts us in all our troubles, so that we can comfort those in any trouble with the comfort we ourselves receive from God"

Sometimes it takes courage to reach out the hand of compassion. Perhaps we tried before and help was rejected, we don't want to get in the way, we don't know what to say in a situation so tragic it's hard to find the right words. However, when we feel His prompting, we should obey remembering He goes with us, His love flows through us and He can give us the wisdom what to do, say or write at a particular time.

Father as You show compassion to us, help us to show compassion to those around us. Help us not to be so caught up in our own lives that we miss the distress flare above the boat of another. Open our eyes today to the needs around us and give us the courage to reach out with the hand of compassion. *"Let no one ever come to you without leaving better and happier. Be the living expression of God's kindness: kindness in your face, kindness in your eyes, kindness in your smile."*— *Mother Teresa*

Replenish – Spending time with God

Pesto is very popular in our house. As a result, there are six little basil plants sitting on the kitchen window sill. This morning they all look slightly sorrowful as have been stripped bare over the last couple of days. There are times in our lives where we have been giving to those around us, seasons where others seem to be picking from us. Maybe they have plucked physical help, babysitting, cooking, lifts, a house move, house renovations. Perhaps, it has been in the soulish area – loved ones have been going through struggles or a volcano has erupted in their lives. For those in ministry, it could be very easy to become like one of my basil plants, due to many demands coming from multiple sources.

Mark 1v35

"Very early in the morning, while it was still dark, Jesus got up, left the house and went off to a solitary place, where he prayed. Simon and his companions went to look for him, and when they found him, they exclaimed: "Everyone is looking for you!"

Jesus is our example; He took himself away from the crowds and from dealing with their needs to spend time with His heavenly Father. We can follow His example by taking ourselves away and spending time with our heavenly Father, being replenished. Even if means that "everyone is looking for us". After time spent with Him, we are better able and equipped to deal with the "everyone's". My empty basil plants after sitting on the sunny windowsill and being watered daily, will be replenished. In a few days the now empty stalks will have green pungent leaves on them, and they'll be ready for the pesto lovers to pluck from them once again.

Luke 5v15 &16

"Yet the news about him spread all the more, so that crowds of people came to hear him and to be healed of their sicknesses. But Jesus often withdrew to lonely places and prayed"

Matthew 14v22&23 "Immediately Jesus made the disciples get into the boat and go on ahead of him to the other side, while he dismissed the crowd. After he had dismissed them, he went up on a mountainside by himself to pray. Later that night, he was there alone"

Father help us today, to make a conscious effort, if we are not already doing it to take time away from the "everyone's" to spend time with You. As we spend time in Your presence, please replenish us so that we are ready to be a blessing to those who want to pluck from us physically, mentally or spiritually today.

Piggy back – Help from our Father

Little legs tired from walking or exhausted from running and the owner pleads "carry me please Daddy". Their Dad kneels down, the young child climbs on their back, wraps their arms around their father's neck, rests their head on his shoulder and lets their father carry them. Many sons or daughters have been carried when tired, weary, weak or in pain. Perhaps some can relate to the child today and are feeling weary, in pain or weak.

Matthew 11v28-30

"Come to me, all who labour and are heavy laden, and I will give you rest. Take my yoke upon you and learn from me, for I am gentle and lowly in heart, and you will find rest for your souls. For my yoke is easy, and my burden is light"

At times, it's not our physical body that is weary. Matthew 11 promises we will find rest for our souls, when we come to Him. Today, you may be worn out from dealing with an awkward colleague or an unappreciative boss. Perhaps you are exhausted from worrying about a wayward child. You may be living in an ice-cold or stressful marriage. There are many situations that can leave us physically exhausted, drained or mentally depleted. He is inviting us to "come to Him" to-day.

Psalm 18v3

"The Lord is my rock, and my fortress, and my deliverer; my God, my strength, in whom I will trust; my buckler and the horn of my salvation and my high tower"

The situation for the small child with didn't change when he thought or talked about his sore legs, nor when he cried and complained about them. He found rest when he came to his Daddy and asked for help.

2 Corinthians 12v9

"But he said to me, "My grace is sufficient for you, for my power is made perfect in weakness"

Father for anyone reading this who's physically tired or mentally weary unsure how to go on, feeling they won't make it, may they come to You today with outstretched arms and simply say "Daddy carry me, through this season please, for I haven't the strength to do it on my own".

Special care units - New Christians

Driving or walking in the countryside in Spring I love watching the young lambs full of the joys of the season, dancing, leaping, then refuelling by drinking from their mothers. Visiting my cousins farm when my children were small, they got opportunities to bottle feed some lambs. The ones who needed extra care and to be hand reared.

Most new-born babies are placed straight into their mothers' arms after birth. Some new-borns, for different reasons have to be cared for in the special care baby unit. The Bible likens new Christians to new born babies, the majority are like the lambs running around the field or the baby handed to its mother. They grow and mature quickly. However, there are some new Christians, who require extra care, a season in the special care unit.

In the special care baby units, specially trained nurses care for the babies, some sick, others premature and very tiny. These nurses don't tell the babies under their care to "buck up, drink and be like the ten-pound baby down the corridor", who guzzles down his milk and roars for more. Rather these nurses rejoice at each new mile stone reached by the babies under their care, until they are able to be discharged from special care.

1 Peter 2v2

"Like new-born babies, crave pure spiritual milk, so by it you may grow up in your salvation"

Perhaps in our circle of influence we know "new-borns" who require extra care, time and attention. We can learn from the nurses in the special care units or the farmer with his hand reared lambs and be patient, exhibit gentleness and rejoice as each milestone is reached. We may have to resist the urge to get frustrated with these new-borns or to compare them to others who seem to be progressing quicker. The time comes, for the hand reared lamb to be let out to play in the field, and the baby to be discharged from special care. The day will come when the baby Christian will be strong enough and adept enough to feed themselves.

1 Corinthians 3v2

"I gave you milk to drink, not solid food; for you were not yet able to receive it. Indeed, even now you are not yet able"

Father help us to have patience with new Christians who need extra care and attention. Give us the wisdom and guidance how to help these people. Help us not to give up on them if the process seems to be taking too long or if there are multiple setbacks along the way.

Jump start – Help one another

At times vehicles are parked up for extended periods of time. Some of these vehicles when their owners try to start them, don't oblige. The key turns in the ignition, but nothing happens. The battery is flat. Sometimes we can relate to the car that won't start. Someone reading this today may be feeling a bit "flat". At times we know the reason for feeling like this but at other times it's not as obvious. When faced with a flat car battery we normally engage the help of another. We ask a passer-by can they oblige by giving the car a push or we find someone who has a set of jump leads.

Galatians 6v9

"Bear one another's burdens and so fulfil the law of Christ"

We are called to bear one another's burdens. When we are having a "flat" day, or week we can ask a brother or sister in the Lord for help. They can give us a push start by praying for us or a jump start by sharing encouraging truths with us. Down the road, when our "flat" battery has been recharged, we will have opportunities to help jump start someone else by praying or giving encouragement. Sometimes, the mere sharing of a burden we are carrying, with someone we trust, can lighten our load.

Colossians 1v92

"And so, from the day we heard, we have not ceased to pray for you, asking that you may be filled with the knowledge of his will in all spiritual wisdom and understanding"

The apostle Paul told the Colossians that he was praying for them. But he tells the Ephesians to pray for all the saints, but also to pray for him.

Ephesians 6v18&19

"Praying at all times in the Spirit, with all prayer and supplication. To that end, keep alert with all perseverance, making supplication for all the saints, and also for me, that words may be given to me in opening my mouth boldly to proclaim the mystery of the gospel."

Father, I pray for anyone reading this today who may be feeling like the car with the flat battery. Please give them courage to reach out and ask someone to help bear their burdens. For those reading this who are driving with fully charged batteries, please Lord put people across their paths in this season who are in need of a jump start.

On average – choosing our words carefully

On average a person speaks many thousand words a day. Imagine if we were to stop and think carefully about each word before we uttered it, like each word in a best man's speech or a teaching. If we did this what percentage of our words would be stopped before they were released?

Psalm 141v3

"Set a guard over my mouth Lord, keep watch over the door of my lips"

How different would we sound if we prayed daily that the Lord would put a guard over our mouths and would keep watch at the door of our lips? Most households have three external rubbish bins and we have become experts at keeping the recycling out of the general bin and throwing the vegetable peelings into the compost bin.

Ephesians 4v29

"Do not let any unwholesome talk come out of your mouths, but only what is helpful for building others up according to their needs, that it may benefit those who listen"

If we were to sort through our words like the household rubbish, which of our words today would make it into the "wholesome" category and which would be classified as "unwholesome"? We can influence others with our words when speaking truth. We can build someone up with encouraging words, we can offer advice with wise words or use our mouths to explain and teach knowledge. Equally, we can affect others when we engage in a battle of words and tear them down. We can tarnish another's reputation by speaking or passing on slander, lies, gossip or fake news.

We can affect another's opinion of themselves, especially a young person with our words. We are called to build up the young people in our lives, not tear them apart. When behaviours need correcting, the child needs to understand it is the "what" and not the "who". Constant criticism or berating, cruel, harsh, heartless words spoken in frustration or in fits of rage can play back on repeat. Perhaps today is the day to start making amends for words hastily spoken and later regretted.

Proverbs 15v23

"A man has joy by the answer of his mouth, and a word spoken in due season, how good it is"

Today, let us be people who speak words in due season.

Proverbs 12v18 - "The words of the reckless pierce like swords, but the tongue of the wise brings healing"

Perhaps – Meditating on the word

When in Spain and planning a day's excursion, one is almost 100 percent certain of what the weather will do, give or take a few degrees in temperature, there are few uncertainties and planning is straightforward.

Back home in Ireland is another scenario completely. For while the day might begin cloudy, "perhaps" it will be raining by lunchtime. There's a "possibility" that the sun may make an appearance, but there's a high "probability" that the wind will be so strong that even your wind breaker won't protect you and "maybe, just maybe" you will have to race home after being drenched by an icy hail shower before you get to even light the barbeque.

Currently there are "many maybes", who like to hang out with the "plenty of perhaps", then "the uncountable uncertainties" plus all the "possibilities to ponder" start a debate. "Probability" rocks up to do the maths and starts to make "predictions" on what the probability is, of the perhaps, the possibilities and the maybes, becoming realities.

Too much meditation on all the perhaps' which means uncertainty or possibility can cause undue anxiety.

Psalm 1v1-3

"Blessed is the man...whose delight is in the law of the Lord, and who meditates on his law day and night. That person is like a tree planted by streams of water, which yields its fruit in season and whose leaf does not wither – whatever they do prospers"

For some it is during the night that "plenty of perhaps" show up, shouting loudly and causing havoc with sleep.

Psalm 63v6

"When I remember You on my bed, I meditate on You in the night watches"

Father, today help me not to spend undue amounts of time pondering on the probability of the perhaps' and the maybes that possibly might happen. But help me to meditate on Your word, which is true; a sure and firm foundation.

Room to grow – **Embracing the new**

Recently, I was in Stillorgan shopping centre, there is a particular shop where we were brought as children for our new shoes. Feet were measured, boxes of shoes brought out, shoes taken out from the tissue paper and tried on. We examined how they looked in the mirrors, walked up and down to see how they felt and the attendant would feel the shoes to check if they were a good fit. Old shoes were boxed up and we danced out of the shop in our new shoes, trying not to scuff them.

There are some small children who leave shoe shops crying, for while there might have been great excitement at the prospect of buying new shoes, they aren't enjoying the reality. The leather is hard, the shoes feel tight, they beg to be allowed to put back on their old shoes.

A small child doesn't understand that wearing shoes that are too small could stunt the growth of their feet as well as affect their posture. We probably all remember the sensation, when trying on new shoes, of the attendant pushing their thumb down on the top of the shoe to ensure "there was room for the foot to grow." New shoes were always bought with "room to grow" space in them.

Isaiah 43v18

"Do not remember the former things, nor consider the things of old. Behold I will do a new thing. Now it shall spring forth, shall you not know it? I will even make a road in the wilderness and rivers in the dessert"

There are times in our walk with the Lord, that He is trying to direct us to the "new" but we like the small child are trying to cling onto the "old". The "old" way, like the old shoes is both familiar and comfortable. In order for us to embrace the new, we have to let go of the old. The "old" could be affecting our posture and stunting our growth. When the small child sticks with the uncomfortable new shoes, the leather eventually softens out, their new shoes mould to the shape of their feet and soon they are walking, running, dancing, skipping, hopping, jumping and kicking a ball without thinking about it.

Father, help me to let go of the old, familiar and comfortable in order to be able to fully embrace the new. While there may be a season where the new feels hard and uncomfortable like the leather in new shoes. If I stick with it, there will not only be opportunities to be stretched and for growth but also the leather will soften out.

The piñata - Don't quit praying

The brightly coloured piñata dangles above the child's head. He picks up the stick and hits on target but there is no obvious effect on the piñata which twirls and twists around. Sometimes it can feel as if our praying is like the little boy hitting the piñata. No results can be seen with our physical eyes. The boy hits the piñata again and again, until his arms grow weary, so he summons the help of another. James 5v18 says that "The prayer of a righteous person is powerful and effective." Just because things may appear the same after we have prayed, we need to not quit like the little boy with his pinata. James 5 tells us that our prayers are both powerful and effective. Sometimes we need to summon in the help from another, for there is great power in the prayer of agreement.

Deuteronomy 32v30

"One man will chase a thousand and two will chase ten thousand"

Suddenly there is a cracking sound above the boy's head and the blessings that were concealed within the Piñata tumble down around him, shrieks of joy fill the air. Maybe we have prayed and prayed for the salvation of a loved one, or a wayward child, or a difficult relationship, or our marriage, for a new home, to be married, for a baby, or a visa application, or about a financial need and nothing appears to have changed and we are tempted to quit. In Joshua 6 we read that the gates of Jericho were securely barred, and no one went in or out. The Lord gave Joshua instructions on what to do in order to take the city of Jericho. For six days, they followed the Lord's instructions and on the morning of the seventh day, they were still looking at Jericho, "securely shut up", nothing seemed to have changed. Then on the seventh day and on the seventh time around there was a suddenly.

Joshua 6v20

"When the trumpets sounded, the army shouted, and at the sound of the trumpet, when the men gave a loud shout, the wall collapsed"

If you are feeling disheartened about a situation that doesn't appear to have changed, take heart, don't quit praying, ask another to come into agreement with you in prayer and expect the suddenly like the Piñata breaking open or the walls of Jericho coming crashing down.

Father help me not to quit praying even when in the natural, nothing appears to have changed or to be happening.

69

Lead by example – Train up a child

I have passed a couple countless times in Castletown parklands, where I walk. Shopping bag in one hand, picker upper in other for the litter. Today was different, I have only ever seen them with their collie. Today, a young lady was with them, she too carrying a litter picker upper.
They no doubt had explained to her what they do, told her tales about how they walk the parklands picking up rubbish left by others. They have shared their enthusiasm for what they do, but today she was getting "on the job training".

Proverbs 22v6

"Train up a child in the way he should go and when he is old, he will not turn from it"

Like the scout leader who doesn't just tell the young cub how to tie knots, he shows him how to do it or the sailing instructor who doesn't only give verbal lessons on dry ground, but demonstrates in a boat on open waters. Training our children in the way they should go, doesn't mean simply telling them. It is training by doing. It includes leading by example. The primary responsibility for training children lies with their parents or guardians. However, there are many others who help in this role and have an important part to play. These include teachers, youth and children's leaders, aunts, uncles, grandparents, coaches etc.

It is pointless telling young people to walk in love unless they see it modelled by us. We can teach them about honesty but are they observing us walking in integrity? We can instruct young people to forgive but do they see us forgiving others, even when it's hard? We can quote Ephesians 6v2 on honouring our parents but what are they observing in this department, for honour, a heart attitude, is for life? We can teach about prayer but do they hear us pray, we can encourage them to read their bibles, but have they seen us? We can tell them to be kind, but what acts of kindness do they observe us doing? We can tell them not to be scared, but what are they hearing come out of our mouths? Being trained in something means observing others and then doing oneself. Many of life's training opportunities come not at pre-selected and scheduled times but rather as situations arise and as things happen.

Help us today Lord to not let an opportunity pass by to train up a child or a young person in the way they should go, in the big matters of life but also in the tiny, seemingly insignificant things where we are modelling Godly character. Where we have missed it in the past, please give us opportunities to rectify our mistakes.

Drifting - Anchoring our minds

When a boat is out on the water and the engine is turned off, the sail down or the oar or paddle abandoned, the boat doesn't stay still or remain in the one place. It will start to drift. Which direction the boat goes in, isn't determined by the person in the boat, but by the winds and currents.

"Absence of mental anxiety" and "the state of not being annoyed by worry" - these are two dictionary definitions for the word peace. Who doesn't want to be in a place of not being annoyed by worry or of being free of mental anxiety?

Isaiah 26v3

"You will keep him in perfect peace"

God promises to keep us, not just in peace but in perfect peace. The next part of the verse is the key. "Whose mind is stayed on you."

Our minds can be like the boat out on the water with no anchor, drifting wherever the wind and currents takes it. The higher the wind, the more it drifts. If the person in the boat doesn't like the direction the boat is heading in, they take back control and start rowing, paddling or steering the boat in the desired direction. When the boat is where they want it to be, they anchor or tie the boat up to prevent it drifting.

We have to choose to keep our mind stayed on Him and not let it drift with the currents or be tossed around by the winds. We can anchor our minds unto His promises. The last part of Isaiah 26v3, tells us why we can, because our trust is in Him.

"You will keep him in perfect peace, whose mind is stayed on you, because he trusts in you"

This is a truth too good to be kept to oneself, why not find at least one person to share it with today?

Father help me to keep my mind stayed on You today, knowing that when I do You will keep me in perfect peace. Please give me opportunity today to share this truth with someone who would benefit from hearing it. In Jesus' name I pray.

Toothpaste tube - **Keep going**

The toothpaste appears empty. You roll up the bottom of the tube and squeeze it hard, a line of stripy toothpaste appears on your toothbrush.

Have you ever felt empty, as though there is nothing left in the tube to give - in a relationship, in ministry or in work? You feel like replacing the "tube".

Sometimes, it's not the time for a new "tube" but time to roll the current one and squeeze what you can from the corners. A squeeze of patience, a squeeze of perseverance, a squeeze of unconditional love, a squeeze of resolve, a squeeze of understanding, a squeeze of forgiveness and a big squeeze of resilience.

We don't need to be too quick to quit at a time when He is directing us to stick.

There is a slogan going around, I saw it on multiple lamp posts during a recent campaign, one about "choice" but unfortunately no consideration was given to the consequences of this choice on another.

If tempted to bin the "tube" we need to consider the domino effect of our choice. What will binning of the tube set in motion and how will it affect the dominoes lined in front of us?

Sometimes we just need to keep rolling the "tube" and squeezing the corners, until He gives the release and says "time for a new tube". And in the meantime, take courage and encouragement from knowing that He is with us, no matter how hard or unpleasant the situation.

Joshua 1v9

"Have I not commanded you. Be strong and courageous. Do not be afraid, do not be discouraged, for the Lord your God will be with you wherever you go".

2 Corinthians 12v9

"But he said to me, "My grace is sufficient for you, for my power is made perfect in weakness"

Father help me to keep rolling the tube until You give the release that it's time for a new tube!

By name – Name not a number

I wrote a story set during the war, so my son bought me a book as part of my Mother's Day gift. "The tattooist of Auschwitz"; based on the true story of Lale Sokolov, one of the tattooists in Auschwitz. In Auschwitz you were stripped of your name, known only by a number. Perhaps it was easier to justify actions towards a number rather than a named individual?

In Gods family, as in our natural families, we aren't mere numbers. We are not simply child number two or child eleven. As the song says, "He knows my name".

Isaiah 43v1

"But now thus says the Lord, he who created you, Oh Jacob, he who formed you Oh Israel, "Fear not I have redeemed you, I have called you by name, you are mine".

He knows each of our names. He knows my name. He knows your name. He is interested in the intimate, intricacies of our lives, every tiny detail of them. We are not just a number to Him.

When we talk about churches and ministries, we often talk numbers. But we need to remember that each of these numbers, is an individual whom He has called by name, whom He sent His son to die for, whom He loves, whom He has a plan for.

In families in the natural, people sometimes say things like "middle child syndrome - the overlooked middle child or the "spoilt baby - the youngest". In Gods family, there are no pampered children, no over looked child, no forgotten child. He knows the name of each of His children and loves each one of us.

John 10v14

"I am the good shepherd; I know my sheep and my sheep know me"

Father thank You that I am not a mere number in the kingdom but You know me and have called me by name."

Elephant Ears - Gossip

I love to watch elephants. Think of the size of their huge, flat, flappy ears. Imagine if our ears were that size, what would our ability to hear be? Many sounds, noises and voices come our way on a daily basis, we hear much and we have choices what to do with what we hear. Half-truths, mistruths, slanted news. What do we do with it? My daughter puts great effort into her college assignments referencing all her sources. Any good scholar knows they can't write something that they think is true, they have to back it up. It's not sufficient to state or write "somebody said". How often do we hear information about another that it seems to come blowing on the wind, no one quite sure from where it originated? An elephant sucks up water with its trunk, sometimes not to drink but rather uses his trunk like a hose and sprays the water out. Some of us need to be like the elephant, sucking up water and hosing down gossip sparks that are coming our way. Little sparks can quickly become big fires. Fires which rage wildly and out of control are hard to extinguish.

Proverbs 16v28

"A perverse person stirs up conflict, and a gossip separates friends"

Proverbs 11v9

"With their words, the godless destroy their friends, but knowledge will rescue the righteous"

Proverbs 11v13

"A gossip betrays a confidence, but a trustworthy person keeps a secret"

Another version says it this way, "a gossip reveals a secret". As it says in Proverbs, friendships have been destroyed by a gossip. Trust has been broken, when something shared in confidence is passed on without permission. In times past, information was harder and slower to spread. Think of how far we have come from when urgent news written in a telegram was delivered to the recipient's door on horseback. Nowadays, a few clicks of a button and private information quickly becomes public and, in an instant can be received on the other side of the globe.

Father help us to be discerning. When news and views come our way, in our homes, classrooms, work places, churches, communities or online, help us to check out the source before passing it on. Dosing any suspect sparks that have the potential to turn into raging fires destroying people's confidence or reputation or burning up relationships.

Be prepared - Salvation

Anyone who was in the scouts knows the motto "Be prepared". This motto devised by the founder of the scouts Balden Powell in 1907. I planted daffodils bulbs in pots and window boxes in preparation, to avoid having empty pots and window boxes in the next season. Deep under the soil, I placed them, to withstand the harshness of winter.

People prepare for retirement by paying into pension funds, to ensure they don't have empty bank accounts in that season of their lives. The squirrel scuttled in front of us on our Autumn walk, mouth full, preparing for the upcoming season.

How many make plans throughout their lives? They may have many details mapped out, but yet have failed to plan for their exit from this life. It has become fashionable to plan one's own funeral. Many have songs picked for their funeral ceremony, flowers chosen that they would like on their coffin, accolades written. Yet have they planned for what lies on the other side of the exit door?

Much toil, many hours of labour, much effort can be put into the accumulation and the care of what one day we will leave behind. Someone recently commented on the obvious, but it struck a chord with me, they spoke of driving past someone's family home, the house remains but their friend has left this world.

Matthew 6v19-21

"Do not store up for yourselves treasures on earth, where moths and vermin destroy and where thieves break in and steal. But store up for yourselves treasures in heaven where moths and vermin do not destroy and where thieves do not break in and steal. For where your treasure is, there your heart will be also"

Father today, give me opportunities wherever this day takes me to talk to those I meet about their preparations for when they go through the exit door of life.

Is it, or isn't it? - Thoughts

Faced with a flower bed to weed, the amateur gardener can ask themself - is this a weed or a flower? Do I leave it in the flower bed or do I pull it out? Our minds could be likened to flower beds. Some look like beautifully manicured flower beds. Others have been allowed to run wild becoming overgrown.

The weeds in a flower bed if left untended spoil the beauty of what was planted there. So, they require pulling out. It's not sufficient to simply take the heads off, the weeds will grow back. They need to be pulled up by their roots. Anyone who has cleared a flower bed can vouch some weeds have stubborn roots.

Philippians 4v8

"Finally, brothers and sisters, whatever is true, whatever is noble, whatever is right, whatever is pure, whatever is lovely, whatever is admirable - if anything is excellent or praiseworthy, think about such things"

When faced with the question-weed or flower, let Philippians 4v8 be the litmus test for each and every thought. If it passes the test, we let it in to the flowerbed of our mind but if it doesn't, we should "take it captive and make it obedient to Christ," 2 Corinthians 10v5.

An untended garden can look daunting if viewed as a whole but when the gardener takes up his trowel and with great resolve starts tackling it, one weed or one briar at a time, he can restore a flower bed to its former glory. However, that is not the end of the gardeners work for weeds are persistent and come back again and again. He has to be vigilant to keep it weeded and continue asking himself "weed or flower?"

Father help me to be like the gardener who asks himself weed or flower and then pulls up the weeds. Help me to ask, "is this thought or thought pattern truth or junk." Let me have the strength, resolve and the self-control to deny entry to what I realize is junk, in Jesus' name I pray.

Excuses, Excuses - Obeying the promptings

Met Eireann had got it right with their forecasting of the latest storm and the warnings they gave. I sat writing in a local coffee shop, there was a pop and we were in darkness. A great excuse for all the staff to put their feet up, send the customer's home and take the rest of the day off. But they didn't, instead they found candles and lanterns to light the way for their customers. As a dear friend would say, "the weather was very inclement" when I spotted a cyclist out the car window. This man was not cycling for leisure, pleasure or for health reasons. He had a trailer attached to the bike and the logo on his jacket showed his purpose for being out in the height of the storm. He was the mail man.

How many times have we heard the whisper from heaven or the still small voice prompting us to deliver a message from heaven? Write the letter to say sorry, send a card to encourage another, witness to a family member, knock on an elderly neighbour's door and offer companionship, ring the friend who is struggling, offer practical help to someone overburdened, meet a financial need of another or offer to pray for a sick colleague? Yet, we can look out the window at the weather and find an excuse - no stamp, no time to talk, don't want someone else's "air of heaviness" to rub off on us, can't afford it, not brave enough, don't want our offer rejected and on and on the excuse list could go. When we hear the promptings from heaven may we make the effort and time to reach out to those in our family, churches, work places, neighbourhoods who He is leading us to help.

Proverbs 3v28

"Do not say to your neighbour "come back tomorrow and I will give it to you-when you already have it with you"

We will never have to dig too deep to find an excuse for something we don't want to do or are not comfortable doing. However, let's try to be like the postman in the storm, battling through the elements to deliver the mail, and be one who will obey those promptings and the still small voice, "in spite of" the weather conditions in our own life.

Proverbs 3v27

"Do not withhold good from those who it is due, when it is in your power to act"

Father, please help me to not ignore Your promptings. Grant me the courage to do what You are leading me to do, and equip me to do it.

All your might - **Diligence**

The one person who is never idle in our house is Ariole Airer, in fact there is normally a queue for her help. One load of washing is finished being dried and another load waits to take their place.

She knows her role and function and does it "with all her might". This despite her role being seasonal and weather dependent, for when the sun reappears and the temperatures rise, Ariole Airer will be folded up and put away, her services no longer required.

Some may find themselves in a season that they know is only temporary - a temporary work contract, a stand in position, or a substitution perhaps and therefore, may be tempted to view their role differently to if it was permanent or long term.

We have Ecclesiastes 9v10 to guide us in life, work and ministry - no matter the length of the commitment we have given or the contract we have signed, we are called to do what we do "with all our might".

Ecclesiastes 9v10

"Whatever your hands find to do, do it with all your might"

It's a spiritual principle and one that will reap rewards not just for others but also for self.

Proverbs 10v4

"He who has a slack hand becomes poor but the hand of the diligent makes rich"

Father, whatever my hands find to do at home, work, in ministry or in my community, help me please to do it with all my might.

Morning has Broken - Thankful for today

The young boy stands in awe at the masterpieces hanging on the gallery wall. Ornate frames around them and guarded by security personnel for fear anyone will touch these one off, unique, never to be repeated masterpieces.

His Father explains that they are originals, one off pieces and for that reason of great value. The little boys heart skips a beat, as he thinks of the one off, unique masterpiece that he created in art class last week, that is lying crumbled at the bottom of his satchel beside the squashed banana. And he wonders what value could be put on this unique masterpiece? Would it yield the price of a trip to Disneyland? And he considers it a shame that he shredded so many previous pieces and threw others in the fire, for then he might be looking at boarding a rocket-ship and not just a plane.

I watched the sun begin to rise over the winter landscape, the reflection of it visible on the duck pond where the swans were stretching and thought of the old hymn, Morning has broken.

When we see many prints of the same original masterpiece, we can become so accustomed to them that we don't truly value the original. Today is not a replica, today is a unique day created for us to embrace, enjoy and be thankful for. It has never been lived before and once the clock strikes midnight it will never be lived again. We need therefore to treat today the way "originals" are worthy of being treated and not look at it like a mere "reprint". There is a purpose to each day, let's live today with passion and discover the purpose for today. No two days lived or to be lived are exactly the same, similar perhaps but not identical.

Psalm 118v24

"This is the day the Lord has made; we will rejoice and be glad in it"

Father thank You for today, the day You have made, I chose to rejoice and be glad in it. To embrace it and to live it to the full. This one-off day, that has never been seen before and will never be repeated again.

Overpayment - **Forgiveness**

Have you ever gone to the till to pay a bill in a restaurant or coffee shop, only to be told the bill has already been taken care of? It has already been paid by another. So, we put away our purse, wallet or card. To pay again would be an overpayment.

1 Peter 2v24

"He himself bore our sins in his body on the tree"

Our sin has been paid for. The sins of mankind have been paid for; those who know Him as their saviour and those who don't yet.

Romans 5v8

"While we were still sinners, Christ died for us".

The sins of those we love have been paid for, as have the sins of those who have treated or do treat us despicably. So why do we try at times to charge them for a debt already paid?

John 1v29

"Behold the Lamb of God who takes away the sin of the world"

How often,
Do we want to have our say?
How often,
Do we want to make others pay?
For what they have done?
The hurts they inflicted on us.
When He says,
"I have already paid for their sin"
Don't try and charge again for
What has already been paid.

Father, please bring to mind today, anyone I am "trying to charge for a debt already paid" be they living or dead. Help me to forgive and release them from this debt. And as I pour out forgiveness to others, please pour Your healing oil into any hurts in my heart they may have caused.

Saver or Spender? – Use your gifts

When my twins were very young, I bought them both a packet of sweets when out for a walk. His were gobbled down, while she slowly savoured hers. Arriving home, she got out her tea set and served the still remaining sweets on little ceramic plates. Her twin sat and watched, mouth-watering, eyes glued to the sweets, too polite to take one.

We often hear people referred to as "big spenders" while others are referred to as "great savers". There is a time to save, but how many people I wonder have got the realization on their death bed that they can't bring what they have saved with them where they are going?

Ephesians 4v8

"When he ascended on high, He led captivity captive and gave gifts to men"

God has given each of us gifts. These gifts are for using and as with a gift in the natural are intended to bless the recipient. Our Heavenly Father doesn't want us to be like a man with a stash of gold who takes it out to polish it and count it but never spends it. There is a time to polish one's gifts but then the day comes to use them to be a blessing to others.

How many, as death approached have regretted not using their God given gifts? In the parable of the talents in Matthew 25, we read about the servant who was given five talents and invested his talents, making five more as did the servant who had been given two talents, making two more.

The master's response to both these servants on his return was "well done good and faithful servant, you have been faithful over a little, I will make you ruler over much". The third servant who had been entrusted with one talent, took a different approach and buried his one talent. When his master learnt of his actions, he was none too pleased and gave orders that the one talent he had be taken from him and be given to the servant with ten.

Father, please help us to recognize and use our gifts. Where we have used excuses, such as being too busy, fearful, timid and shy, not proficient in the language of the country we reside, too old, too young and on and on the reasons go, we are sorry. Help us not to always think, "well there is always tomorrow" but rather start using the gifts You have given us today.

In comparison to - Sin

I was not impressed watching the dog take a flying leap over the gate of the contained dog park in pursuit of rabbit scent. The last time she did this, I have just about enough fingers to count the hours she was gone, running up and down a deep ditch and couldn't be caught, such is her speed, agility and determination.

We met a man, while looking for her. He loves beagles. His own two beagles went hunting for three days in the same park. In comparison to this, "our Lily" was an angel.

We can at times compare ourselves to others. Compared to the behaviour of some, we shine so brightly and can hence be tempted to justify our misdemeanours. What is helping oneself to some stationery from the press in work compared to the one who scammed thousands from an innocent victim or robbed a bank? What is one little white lie compared to those who weave beautiful webs of deceit which shine brightly like the spider's web in the dew?

Lily was wrong to run off, even if she didn't clock up the hours of the since deceased two Leixlip beagles. Our standard for self or others should not be measured against the behaviour of those around us, politicians or those we read about in the courts section of the newspaper. Our standard for self should be His standard that we read of in His word.

I have said to the young people in church many times, just because we believe in grace and forgiveness, doesn't mean we don't repent. The wrong answer remains on the copy book page until the student picks up an eraser and rubs it out. We have a loving, forgiving Heavenly Father but we need to utter the words "I am sorry".

1 John 1v9

"If we confess our sins, he is faithful and just and will forgive us our sins and cleanse us from all unrighteousness"

Acts 3v19

"Repent therefore and be converted, that your sins may be blotted out"

Father help me not to judge right and wrong by the behaviour of others around me. Rather help me to look to Your word. Please shine the spotlight on any area of my life that doesn't line up with the way You would want it to. Help me be quick to repent and confess my sins to You when I make a mistake. In Jesus name I pray.

Shattered – **Brokenness**

Sitting outdoors by the embers of an open fire, I was listening to worship from some young people. Two lines from a particular song jumped out at me. "And you picked up all the pieces, put me back together." There is a restoration programme currently on the television. Discarded, no longer used, many not too pretty items make it onto this programme. All have seen better days. Most now sit idle in outhouses, attics, sheds and store rooms. Many of us wouldn't give these pieces a second look, considering their "day to be long past". That is until the restorers, experts in their particular fields, start to work on these broken pieces.

There was a beautiful table with a tell-tale crack running right up the centre through it. The restorer's expertise was tested to the maximum, to ensure no evidence of the crack would be seen in the restored table. He was successful in his endeavours. Our Heavenly Father is the master restorer - of broken dreams, lost hope, cracked relationships, strained emotions or hurting bodies. Expert restorers can make something damaged and broken look "just like new again".

Isaiah 45v18

"Forget the former things, do not dwell on the past. See I am doing a new thing"

A small child goes to their daddy with a broken toy, asking him to fix it. In order for this to happen, they need to place the toy in their father's hands. Similarly, we can bring areas of our lives that need repair and fixing to our Heavenly Father. It might be a simple crack that requires attention, a straightforward dent or it may be more complex. We could be looking at a situation that appears like many tiny pieces and are wondering how they could ever be put back together again.

Jeremiah 30v17

"But I will restore you to health and heal your wounds,' declares the LORD"

Joel 2V25

"I will restore to you the years that the swarming locust has eaten"

Father, thank You that you are the master restorer. I choose to entrust any areas of brokenness in my life into Your loving hands. Please fix, repair and bring healing and wholeness.

Even the Spanish Ants - **Seeking Him**

Anyone who knows my mother-in-law, knows that no matter where you go with her, you will never be disappointed in your search for something sweet to accompany your tea, coffee or soft drink. Into her bag she will reach and find sweet treasure. Even our dog Lily has had the pleasure of discovering and helping herself to a chocolate bar from Nanny's bag.

Upon arriving in a rural part of Spain, Nanny's bag was spotted with a procession of ants climbing their way in. Now if we had coaxed these Spanish speaking ants in, they wouldn't have heeded us but they had smelt out the open chocolate bar at the bottom of the bag. This, not any old bar of chocolate, but a delicious bar of Cadbury's chocolate brought from Ireland.

1 Chronicles 16v11

"Look to the Lord and His strength. Seek His face always"

Jeremiah 29v13

"You will seek me and find me when you seek me with all your heart"

The timeless game of hide and seek has delighted many generations of young people and continues to do so. Those hiding do not want to be found by the seeker. Our Heavenly Father does not play hide and seek with His children nor with those who have yet to know Him as Father. He has promised that those who seek Him will find Him. So, when we hear people say, they are "looking for God" may their searching not be fruitless or in vain.

Proverbs 8v17

"Those who seek me find me"

Father for those seeking and looking, at the end of their search may they find You.

Let's not wallow - **Self-pity**

While pigs don't make it onto my list of top ten favourite animals, it always amazes me when looking into a pig pen to find it not full of clean straw like the horse's stable, but full of mud. Then to observe them not turning up their snouts at the muck but rather wallowing in it - rolling around in it on purpose. I heard the Lord say "don't wallow in self-pity". Pigs wallow in the mud, it sticks to them and is there for all around to see. It's the same for us when we wallow in self-pity, it's often visible to those we spend time with. There's a time to be upset about something that has befallen us but wallowing is "devoting oneself entirely to something or indulging to an immoderate degree" Some definitions say "to seem to enjoy being sad, especially because you get sympathy from other people".

Ecclesiastes 3 tells us there is a season for everything or a time for everything. There is a time to weep and a time to laugh and there is a time to mourn and a time to dance. When bad, sad, unfortunate, unfair things happen to us individually, to our families or our nation, there's a time to weep and be sad. God gave us emotions. However, there comes a time to laugh again. It's okay to laugh once more. Wallowing in self-pity can be detrimental as it blinds us to the needs of others. We were created to be "others centred" but when wallowing in self-pity we can become self-absorbed.

While self-pity can lead some to seek the attention of others for others it can cause them to shut away, isolate themselves, becoming like the iceberg that has broken away and is floating alone. We were created for fellowship, to bless and encourage and to be blessed and encouraged. If we have been wallowing in self-pity, the first thing is to recognize that it's become an issue. Then we need an exchange, taking off the coat of self-pity that we have slipped into and allowing Him clothe us once more with His joy. Let Him fill us up so it bubbles and overflows out of us. Contentment is a decision. It doesn't mean that everything in our world is perfect, but rather we have chosen to be content and thankful in spite of the thorns that grace our rose bushes. Choosing to enjoy the beauty and scent from the roses without our sole focus being on the thorns.

Philippians 4v11

"For I have learned to be content whatever the circumstances"

Father today I repent if I have indulged in self-pity, please forgive me and help me to focus not on the minuses from the past and present but the pluses. Help me to choose to be content, having an attitude of gratitude. If my attention has been inward, help turn it outward.

A Promise - Faith

When a promise is made to a very young child by a loved one, they believe it. They gaily tell everyone they meet about the new bike they have been promised or their favourite ice cream that is going to be bought for them or the trip to the zoo they will be making and they act accordingly. The back pack is filled for the Zoo trip or the old bike given away and they often remind the promise giver of the promise they have made.

Why? Because they believe the promise that was made to them as they trust the person who made it.

Hebrews 11v1

"Now faith is the substance of things hoped for, the evidence of things not yet seen"

Faith is believing and trusting the promises of God. Faith is believing His promises, before we can see the promise manifested, feel it or are experiencing it. Faith has corresponding actions. If we truly believe and trust our Heavenly Father. We are like the small child who has been made a promise, we talk about the promise as a given certainty not as some airy, fairy thing that just might come to pass one day. We believe what He has promised and we plan and act accordingly.

James 2v26, tells us that faith without works is dead.

Father, please help me today to have childlike faith, that trusts Your promises, help me to speak and act accordingly. If a promise has taken longer than I anticipated to come to pass, let me refresh my mind today with the promise that You gave, in Jesus' name I pray.

The Ripple Effect - **Our actions**

A crystal, clear, motionless lake is before you shimmering in the sunshine. You pick up a little pebble and toss it in. It hits the surface of the water and sinks to the bottom of the lake. Small circular ripples spread across the surface of the water.

If our only focus is on the pebble hitting the bottom of the lake, we have missed its true impact. Our words and actions produce ripple effects. Do we give due attention to the ripple effects produced by the words we speak, write and our actions?

What are the ripple effects from the money given on a regular basis to provide for a child, not your own to be educated? In ten years or even twenty years how far will the ripples of your giving have spread? How many other lives will have been affected by your decision in giving towards a child's education, or a feeding programme many times a complete stranger?

Words spoken, have no cost to us, other than our time. What are the ripple effects from words of love spoken to a weary, hurting, downtrodden, discouraged listener, when these words bring encouragement, sparking a flame of hope again? How far do the ripples of these words spread?

There are many things we do on a daily basis that can seem insignificant and mundane, a drudgery even. Yet how far do the ripples from these things travel, across the lives of others? Sometimes, this question will only be answered for us when we get to heaven.

Galatians 6v9&10 – amplified

"Let us not grow weary or become discouraged in doing good, for at the proper time we will reap if we do not give in. So then while we (as individual believers) have the opportunity, let us do good to all people, not only being helpful but also doing that which promotes their spiritual well-being and especially (be a blessing) to those of the household of faith".

Father I pray for the ripple effect from the words of love, truth and encouragement I speak today. I pray for the ripple effect for the good seed I plant into ministries or into the lives of others. I pray for the ripple effect from my deeds today, in Jesus' name.

Smudge Marks – Hold fast to truth

Have you ever felt your vision was distorted or hampered? Only to realize the problem was caused by smudge marks or smears on the lens of your glasses or sunglasses. Sometimes, the way we view things can become distorted or hampered so that we can't see clearly. Smudge marks have appeared in our line of vision. Some people can be very persuasive in their points of view, they can argue eloquently, speak coherently or write passionately. Perhaps this has caused you to even question a belief you held dear, if it's not in-line with the beliefs of the majority.

If your core beliefs don't tally with those of the majority, nowadays you can be labelled many different things. That doesn't mean the minority view isn't correct. Just because the majority of exam candidates, answer an exam question in a particular way, doesn't make it the right answer.

We can be kind, caring, compassionate, non-judgmental and still hold true to the beliefs that we hold dear. When you buy a new pair of sunglasses, oftentimes there are sticky labels that have to be removed. So, if we have been unjustly labelled because of our beliefs, we need to peel away those labels. If others have tried to win us over to their points of view, we need to stand true to our convictions.

1 Corinthians 15v58

"Be steadfast, immovable, always abounding in the work of the Lord".

Father, please highlight any smudge marks in my line of vision. Help me to not to be swayed from the beliefs I hold true, even when they are not the majority view. Help me to be steadfast, immovable and always abounding in the work of the Lord.

Precious pearls – Fixing

My Monasterevin friend regularly shares pearls of wisdom with me. She always starts with, "in my language we have this proverb". For it was far from the fields and horses of Kildare she was born and raised.

One of our own pearls of wisdom says "a stitch in time saves nine". To many younger people, that wouldn't make as much sense as to those raised when things were more readily repaired, fixed and mended.

Sometimes it is easier to stick one's head in the sand like the ostrich, rather than dealing with what is around us that needs dealing with. While this approach may bring temporary relief, nothing changes while our head is stuck in the sand.

Dealing with small credit card debt is easier than when it has increased greatly due to interest. A strained relationship is easier to darn back together than when a huge divide appears causing the relationship to become ripped apart. A situation that needs tackling, a person that needs confronting in love, while tempting to take the ostriches example and gain temporary relief, this is not always the best approach. In the long-term threading the darning needle and making that one stitch is much easier than making those nine down the line.

Father help me today to make those single stitches in areas that require repair, I ask You for the wisdom and the strength to start fixing what needs fixing in Jesus' name.

Psalm 34v17

"The righteous cry and the Lord hears and delivers them out of all their troubles".

The real deal – Truth

The smell of the sweet peas in the Botanical gardens kept drawing me back, to walk past them again and so savour the sweetness of their aroma. It brought me back to my childhood and visits to my Granny's beautiful garden. In summertime there were always sweet peas growing in abundance. Honeysuckle fragrances in the air on a balmy evening or freshly cut grass make us think of summertime and all the good things about it. These are three natural aromas that appeal to me.

We burn scented candles to fill our homes with nice smells, we put on perfumes and colognes. We spray air fresheners from cans. Nice and all, as these smells are, none quite compare to the "real deal", the lavender growing in the garden or the smell from the gorse as we walk past on a hike or fresh mint in the pot on the kitchen windowsill.

When it comes to truth, there is nothing like the "real deal". His word is the "real deal" and anything that tries to replicate might smell nice like the vanilla candle or the new cologne but it's not the real deal. Somethings can be almost right or half right but still not be the "real deal".

Hebrews 4v12

"For the word of God is alive and active. Sharper than any double-edged sword. It penetrates even to dividing soul and spirit, joints and marrow. It judges the thoughts and attitudes of the heart"

Isaiah 55v11

"So is my word that goes out from my mouth: it will not return to me empty, but will accomplish what I desire and achieve the purpose for which I sent it"

Father, please give me discernment. Help me to sniff out when something that is not the real deal is trying to present itself as being the real deal.

Strengthened from within – Rejoicing in hope

Inadvertently you knock the raw egg against a hard surface, causing it to smash. The delicate shell couldn't withstand the force of the knock.

You take another from the box, place it in a saucepan of water and boil it. As it boils the egg knocks off the side of the metal pan but doesn't smash open. It has been hardened from within by the heat.

James 1v2-4

"Consider it pure joy my brothers and sisters whenever you face trials of many kinds. Because you know that the testing of your faith produces perseverance. Let perseverance finish its work so that you may be mature and complete"

While we don't relish the prospect of trials. The heat from these trials strengthens us within like the little egg in the pot of boiling water.

Romans 12v12

"Rejoice in hope, be patient in tribulation, be constant in prayer"

If we feel the scorching heat of a trial burning down on us today and it looks like the forecaster is predicting no change in the days ahead. We can rejoice in the hope that we have in Him, remaining patient and constant in prayer. Confident that one day the weather will break and the intense heat which feels like is going to burn us up, will be replaced by cooler weather.

James 1v12

"Blessed is the man who remains steadfast under trial, for when he has stood the test, he will receive the crown of life which God has promised to those who love Him"

Father help me to remain steadfast when under trial. Help me to rejoice in hope, to be patient in tribulation and to be constant in prayer.

Fail better – Getting back up

When the young people in church were asked to share a fear, they had I was surprised at what made it in to top place. "Fear of failure" came in as number one and linked to it, fear of not reaching other people's expectations. We visited an exhibition in Trinity's science museum a number of years ago, called "Fail Better". There were exhibits and stories of peoples failed attempts in many different endeavours, across a broad spectrum of life. Visitors were encouraged to write their own experiences of failure on the wall.

Nobody likes the word "fail", when it applies to them. Perhaps on a returned exam script or assignment. Who wants to be told "their application has failed to meet the criteria" or "you've failed to meet the requirements for promotion"? Failed relationships, cause pain and heartache, and can make it hard to trust again. Many athletes train hard yet fail to qualify or to be selected. Lifetime savings and many hours of labour have been poured into businesses which subsequently fail. Failure can cause pain, disappointment, discouragement, shame or embarrassment. It can make a person fearful of trying again or engaging in different ventures.

Proverbs 24v16

"For though a righteous man falls seven times he will get up"

Many "failures" come with valuable life lessons attached, which once we have dried our eyes and read them properly, we can learn from. For some the key to success lies in humbling themselves and seeking the advice of others.

Proverbs 15v22

"Plans fail for lack of counsel, but with many advisers they succeed"

Desire alone won't take us to the mountain peak.

Proverbs 12v24

"Diligent hands will rule"

There's only a small window of opportunity each year when climbers are allowed to attempt to scale Everest. Failure sometimes can simply be due to a timing issue. Who wants to buy fleece socks and hot water bottles on a Spanish beach in August?

Fail better – Getting back up

Ecclesiastes 3v1

"There is a time for everything, and a season for every activity under the heavens"

Finally, in some instances, we are within touching distance of success and we just have to keep on going and not quit.

Galatians 6v9

"And let us not grow weary of doing good, for in due season we will reap, if we do not give up"

Father I pray for anyone reading this who has experienced failure. Failure hurts, be it in a marriage, a business venture, a ministry, friendship, exams. Please heal their hearts and don't let the failure define them. May they hope, dream, trust and succeed.

Laced up – Bringing together

I saw this one in a dream. Two ends of a white lace, lying open and apart. They remain so until a pair of hands unites them by picking up the ends and tying a bow in them. Both ends are now working together to reach a common goal.

Tied laces in a shoe or boot help to hold them in place. If the lace remains untied, the shoe doesn't look aesthetically pleasant, the shoe can slip off or the opened shoelaces can pose a safety hazard. Untied shoe laces can cause the owner to stumble, trip up or fall.

Have you ever felt like a lace, totally separated from what, where or who it is meant to be connected to? Sometimes it can look like an impossibility to ever work with a certain individual or to feel part of a particular group. But when the hand of God picks up the separated pieces and unites them, purpose can be fulfilled like the lace in a shoe.

If we allow Him, He can bring together the areas in our lives that are separated, like the two ends of the white lace I saw in my dream. In our homes, in our extended family, with our in-laws, in work, in church and in friend groups.

Ecclesiastes 4v9

"Two are better than one, because they have a good reward for their labour"

Father today, I ask that You pick up any separated ends of my life and make bows where there needs to be bows - bringing together what needs to be brought together and thus stopping me from tripping or stumbling due to any unlaced area in my life. You are the God who says - with Me all things are possible.

Corresponding actions - **Love softens**

In my opinion, you can't beat real butter in a taste test, in spite of not always being practical when trying to spread it straight from the fridge. Sitting in the heat of my kitchen, the rock-hard butter starts to soften and becomes easier to spread or to bake with.

Have you ever met a person, with a heart like my rock, hard, cold butter? People with hard hearts can be hard work on many levels - difficult, unappreciative, rude, arrogant, argumentative and on and on the list could go. As I write I think of my many friends who work in the medical world. At times encountering awkward, rude, difficult, aggressive or unappreciative patients or family members on wards, in clinics or surgeries.

Just like the heat in my kitchen softens the hard butter block, we can trust God, that the heat from His love flowing through us will help melt the hardest heart that crosses our path. Easy spreadable butter alternatives can be more attractive to us but even those with hard hearts need to be exposed to His love.

Mark 12v31

"Love your neighbour as yourself"

It's not enough to simply say we love someone – do we have corresponding actions?

John 3v18

"Dear children, let's not merely say that we love each other, let us show the truth by our actions"

At the last supper, Jesus washed the feet of His disciples. He didn't exclude the one who would deny Him nor the one who would betray Him. He demonstrated His love for His disciples by His actions. Sometimes words can come cheap but backing up the "I love you" with corresponding actions can at times require a dying to self.

Father, today please help me to demonstrate love to those I meet, even those whose hearts appear like a pound of butter straight from the fridge. Father as a vessel of Your love, I trust You to pour your love through me helping to soften the hardest of hearts.

Derailed by disappointment – **Back on the tracks**

Standing on station platforms, waiting passengers hear announcements such as, "stand back, train now approaching" or I recently heard "train passing through". It did so at speed. Nothing though compared to the speed of the bullet trains, the latest to be unveiled, the Alpha-X, capable of reaching speeds of 224mph. A derailed train, travels at 0mph and covers no ground.

We can be traveling at high speed like the bullet train - dreaming, hoping, praying, planning, trusting and waiting expectantly. Then situations prevail. Our train of hope becomes derailed by disappointment. Disappointment defined as – "sadness or displeasure caused by the non-fulfilment of ones hopes and expectations". It can hurt. If we hadn't hoped, hadn't prayed and hadn't trusted, perhaps not as intensely.

Psalm 34v18

"The Lord is near to the broken-hearted and saves the crushed in spirit"

He promises to be near to us when our hearts are broken from the pain of disappointment. He promises to save us if we are crushed in spirit.

Psalm 30v5

"Weeping may last through the night, but joy cometh with the morning"

The derailed train gets lifted back onto the track and starts to operate again. It begins to fulfil purpose again be that in carrying freight or passengers. There comes a time when we have been derailed to allow Him to lift us back onto the tracks again or to climb back on ourselves. We can hope again, dream again, we can trust again. Like the repositioned train we can start to fulfil purpose once again.

Proverbs 55v22

"Give your burdens to the Lord and He will take care of you. He will not permit the Godly to slip and fall"

Father I pray for those reading this today who have been derailed by disappointment. Disappointment hurts. Disappointment can cause us to question. Please comfort them today, let them know You are near. Heal their hearts from this disappointment. Give them the courage to climb back onto the rails again or lift up those too weak to climb so that once more they can fulfil purpose.

Cut off the weights – Laying aside

The small child gazes upward, their face crumples as the realization hits, their precious helium balloon is fast becoming a distant speck. The helium balloon is on an upward course. Little weights which come in a variety of shapes and colours are designed to hold the helium balloon in place and prevent it taking flight. But once the weights are cut off, the balloon is free to rise.

Hebrews 12v1

"Let us lay aside every weight and the sin which so easily ensnares us and let us run with endurance the race that is set before us"

The NIV says let us throw off everything that hinders. Both of these versions require action on our part. "Laying aside" or "throwing off" aren't things that happen by themselves or simply because there is a desire for them to occur.

The weights have to be actively removed from the helium balloon to enable it to rise. So too, we need to actively remove any weights and the sin that "ensnares" or "entangles us".

Have you ever seen a lonesome balloon hanging from the branch of a tree, its' string entangled, preventing the balloon from rising? Hebrews12, talks of the sin that ensnares or entangles us. We can become like the balloon whose string is wrapped around the tree branch, held back and going nowhere.

Periodically it is good to do a self-assessment. To search our hearts and to ask our Heavenly Father, if there are weights that we have been carrying or if sin has ensnared or entangled us.

Father, please show me today any unnecessary weights that I have been needlessly carrying so I can lay them down. Shine Your light on any sin that may have ensnared me so that I can repent of it. Father I want to run with endurance the race that You have set before me and not be held back.

Leaving the shore – **Offense**

Standing on the cliff on a warm summer's day, the cove below is awash with activity. Small boats take to the waters. Some Christians have left the shore in boats. Some have not picked up oar or paddle or raised their sails but the wind of busyness and the waves of other commitments have caused their boats to drift away from the shoreline of fellowship. Others, have jumped into a little fishing boat, the timber name plaque boasting the word "Offended" in blue paint, they have chugged from the harbour and are yet to return to fellowship.

Proverbs 18v19

"A brother offended is more unyielding than a strong city"

"Or harder to be won" is how another version puts it. The second half of this verse says "arguments separate friends like a gate locked with bars". In Luke 17, Jesus warned His disciples that offenses will come. Unfortunately, no one is born with a natural immunity and there is no vaccination that we can get against offense. Offenses will come and the reasons for them are as varied as the shapes of the dainty shells decorating the sand at the water's edge. It's what we do, when these offenses come that matters. Castles of old were built with defence measures in place for the expected enemy. We can be prepared for when offense comes.

Psalm 119v165

"Great peace have they which love thy law and nothing shall offend them"

While opportunities to get offended will come, we can determine not to take offense. We have all met people that are carrying offenses from actions done to them weeks, months, years or even decades ago. At times we can be guilty of picking up the offense of others, because of hurts caused to them. Today may be the day to rip up or burn some record sheets and let the healing process begin.

1 Corinthians 13v5 "Love keeps no record of being wronged."

Father, please show me if I am carrying offense. I chose to forgive those who I am offended at. If I have picked up the offense of another, I choose to lay it down.

Everlasting – Love of God

Some people love watching advertisements and are great at recounting old ones that are firmly lodged in their memory. I, on the other hand "switch over", "switch off" or "switch on" the kettle when advertisements appear on the television.

Yet drummed into my brain, is the idea that a particular brand of battery is king of the battery world and go on and on and on. Of course, this isn't the case and the light from the battery-operated torch will eventually grow dim and the beeping smoke detector alerts you to replace the battery.

The concept of everlasting is sometimes hard to grasp in a world where everything runs its course. However, we are promised that His love for us is everlasting. It is never going to grow dim, it will never run dry, it doesn't run out and it will never beep to warn us to go in search of a different source of love.

Jeremiah 31v3

"I have loved you my people with an everlasting love. With unfailing love, I have drawn you to myself".

Psalm 143v8

"Cause me to hear Thy loving kindness in the morning; for in Thee do I trust; cause me to know the way wherein I should walk; for I lift my soul unto Thee"

Peoples love for us may have run out or come up short but we can take heart today knowing that His love towards us endures forever. How long is forever? Forever.

Psalm 136v26

"Give thanks to the God of heaven. His love endures forever"

Father help me to grasp the fact that Your love towards me is everlasting. That it is not going to suddenly run out.

Fan vs Follower – True followers

I listened to the young man teaching the teenagers, him a teenager himself. He challenged them, talking about "fans" and "followers". When we think of "fans" depending on our age, different images spring to mind. My generation of fans, stuck posters of their favourite artists on their bedroom walls and dreamt of having an opportunity to get signatures in an autograph book. A fan is one who has admiration for another.

In Matthew 16v24 Jesus said "if anyone would come after me, let him deny himself and take up his cross and follow me". Jesus is looking for "followers" and not just "fans". Being a fan doesn't require the same level of commitment as a follower does. Fans of a particular team enjoy watching their team play, followers will go a step further and incur expense by doing whatever it takes to follow that team to stadiums at home and abroad.

In the childhood game, "follow the leader", the actions of the person leading the game are mimicked. A follower is called to mimic.

John14v12

"Whoever believes in me, will do the works I have been doing and they will do even greater works"

The rich young ruler in Mark 10 told Jesus that he had obeyed the commandments since his youth but Jesus exhorted him in verse 21 to come and follow Him. This was a heart and commitment issue. As followers of Him, we are not interested in writing fan mail but rather in reading instructions from His word and listening in that quiet place to the specific instructions that He has for each of His followers.

Matthew 4v19

"Come follow me and I will make you fishers of men"

Father help me never to want to opt for the easier path of being a fan but rather to commit to being a true follower.

Roundabout moments - **Direction**

The roundabout is before you, offering a choice of multiple exits. You sail through it without any thought, for you know your destination and the necessary route to get there. Sometimes we can feel like we are facing an imaginary roundabout in our life. Other times we can feel almost dizzy from driving around and around the same roundabout multiple times, unsure of which exit to take.

When we use sat navs or google maps on our phone as we approach a roundabout, a voice tells us, multiple times, which exit off the roundabout to take. When we are tuned in, listening and not distracted we hear the voice on the sat nav.

Isaiah 30v21

"Whether you turn to the left or the right, your ears will hear a voice behind you saying this is the way walk in it"

At times the voice of the sat nav can be drowned out by other voices in the car. Or the directions it gives can be ignored in favour of a better route in the driver's opinion.

If you are facing a roundabout decision today or if you are dizzy from indecisiveness. Take heart. Trust Him to clearly lead you and guide you which is the best exit to take and then follow His instruction.

Psalm 32v8

"I will instruct you and teach you in the way you should go, I will counsel you with my eye upon you"

Isaiah 48v17

"Thus, says the Lord, your Redeemer, the Holy one of Israel. "I am the Lord your God, who teaches you to profit, who leads you in the way you should go"

Father, when facing roundabout decisions, with many options but unsure which one to take, please lead and guide me which exit to take.

Nest building – Home

The sun was shining. The air was clear and the skies overhead were full of birdsong. From each bush and tree there was a different note being sung. It was beautiful to listen to. As I reached the end of my walk, I spotted a blackbird on the path ahead. He wasn't joining in the singing, for a bundle of tiny twigs was being carried, in his vibrant orange beak. A scripture sprang to mind from Matthew 6. "Look at the birds of the air, they do not sow or reap or store away in barns and yet your Heavenly Father feeds them. Are you not much more valuable than they? Who of you by worrying can add a single hour to his life?" The blackbird wasn't stressed, anxious or worried about where the next twig would be found to build his nest with, or if there would be enough rabbit fur to line the nest with to keep his chicks warm. He wasn't concerned either that he wouldn't be able to find a suitable place to build his nest and birds have no concerns about deposits, mortgages or down payments.

For many in the current climate in Ireland the finding of a new place to live can be problematic. In the natural, this could cause stress when one wonders where they can find to build a nest. Will there be a tree in the right location and will the rental of the tree not be exorbitant? Will the tree owner offer them a branch to rent or will he/she give preference to someone else? We have a loving heavenly Fathers who says in Matthew 6v25 "Do not worry about your life, what you will eat or drink or about your body what you will wear. Is not life more important than food and the body more important than clothes?"

V 28 - 33 "And why do you worry about clothes? See how the lilies of the field grow. They do not labour or spin. Yet I tell you that not even Solomon in all his splendour was dressed like one of these. If this is how God clothes the grass of the field, which is here today and tomorrow is thrown into the fire, will he not much more clothe you? Oh, you of little faith. So do not worry saying "What shall we eat?" or "What shall we drink?" or "What shall we wear?" "But seek first His kingdom and His righteousness and all these things shall be given to you as well. Therefore, do not worry about tomorrow"

We thank God that He has taken care of all our tomorrows and today we chose not to worry about our physical needs but rather to enjoy this day He has made for us.

Father for anyone reading this who is in the process of nest building, I pray You lead, guide, direct, provide and grant them favour.

Grasp – Love of God

When a child first goes to a swimming pool to learn to swim; measurements are everything. Is he near enough the side of the pool to cling on to it with both hands? Can her feet touch the bottom of the pool? As she progresses, there is a sense of satisfaction when able to swim a width and make it to the far side of the pool. The sounds of the children in the water echo off the high roof. The bather is allowed to swim in the deep end, where no longer can their toes feel the security of ground beneath them, googles on, they master a full length of the pool. Everything is about measurements.

I awoke this morning and heard the word "grasp".

Ephesians 3v18

"And may you have the power to grasp how wide and how long and high and deep is the love of Christ"

His love for us is immeasurable - the height of it, the depth of it, the length of it and the width of it.

Some struggle with the love of God, due at times to their own past failings and feelings of unworthiness. Others have been treated so vilely by others and made to feel so little of, that it can be hard to comprehend the magnitude of His love for them. They feel unworthy of it.

He is love, and His love for us is unmerited, unconditional and eternal. He doesn't blow hot and cold. He was love yesterday, He is love today and He will be love tomorrow.

Psalm 86v5

"You Lord are forgiving and good, abounding in love to all who call to you".

In Psalm 136, we read His steadfast love endures forever.

Bask in the width, depth, height and length of the love of Your Heavenly Father today.

The orchestra - Unity

Sitting in the classroom, the sunlight streaming in the big bay windows. Following along with our pencils on the music score as classical music filled the room. I am not sure if we, fourteen-year-old girls, shared in the teacher's excitement for classical music. Brought to the National concert hall to experience this music live, rather than listening to it being played on the little school cassette player to further wet our appetites. Those and my dad playing it at home are my memories of being introduced to classical music.

Each of us probably has a favourite instrument, and maybe a favourite part of the orchestra. When the sounds of the woodwind, strings, brass, percussion mix together to use a cliché – it's music to our ears! What if one musician decides to play at the wrong tempo or another hasn't really practiced and doesn't know the piece? What if the flute player decides to ignore the leading of the conductor? Even though the rest of the orchestra is playing as one, our attentions are drawn to the one musician that is playing off. It affects the overall sound and enjoyment for the listener.

Psalm 133v1,3

"Behold how good and how pleasant it is for brethren to dwell together in unity! It is like the precious ointment upon the head...for there the Lord commands the blessing"

How good and how sweet when we dwell in unity - whether in our families both immediate and extended, churches, classrooms, places of work, committees, teams, friend groups etc. Where there is unity, the Lord commands a blessing. Unity doesn't mean we agree with every idea and point of view. Rather unity means the absence of strife. Strife is deadly. It has the ability not only to spread but also to open the door to its friend bitterness and the window to its buddy unforgiveness.

James 3v16

"For where envying and strife is, there is confusion and every evil work".

Proverbs 20v3

"It is to one's honour to avoid strife, but every fool is quick to quarrel"

Father help each one reading this be determined to keep strife out. Where strife has already wedeled its way in, help them to resolve the issues causing it so that unity can be restored, in Jesus' name I pray.

Little porridge pot - Giving

Many of us have memories of books from our childhood. Illustrated books that captured our imagination. Stories that were read to us and others by us, that have remained firmly lodged in our memories. Characters we found inspiring. Books crammed with interesting facts. Quirky and funny stories that made us laugh and then those that gave us lumps in our throats. If I asked for favourites, probably no two would be the same. An image, that sticks in my memory is of the little porridge pot. The pot on the stove started to bubble over, the porridge dripped onto the stove, then onto the floor and then out the front door of the house and down the street it went. The porridge pot bubbling with provision.

Luke 6v38

"Give and it will be given to you. Good measure, pressed down, shaken together and running over. Will be poured into your lap. For with the measure you use, it will be measured to you"

Sometimes we think by holding on and amassing that we will have more. In Gods kingdom the opposite is the case, when we give willingly - not reluctantly or under compulsion (or the NLT says in response to pressure) we will be richer for it on many levels.

Proverbs 11v24

"One gives freely and grows all the richer, another withholds what he should give and only suffers want"

Neighbours came and filled their pots with the porridge that was running down the street and the little porridge pot kept on bubbling and kept on overflowing. I just love that image. Not only were the needs of the household met but also those of others. God gives us bread to eat and seed to sow. We need balance, not to give away the bread He gives as our provision and also not to keep what He has given us to sow - 2 Corinthians 9v10. Maybe you have had a burning desire to help loved ones or to help those in need but always feel you can't afford to.

2 Corinthians 9v8

"And God will generously provide all you need. Then you will always have everything you need and plenty left over to share with others"

Father thank You for Your provision today. Thank You for the desire and ability to be a giver and thus be a blessing to others.

105

Making plans - Trust

When a loved one, living abroad makes contact and lets you know they are coming on a trip home, you start to plan. You prepare a room, fill the fridge, clear your diary and start the countdown. The sense of anticipation and excitement mount. You believe what they have told you and you act accordingly.

We say it, write it, sing it, in many different ways but basically when translated they all mean the same thing i.e. "I believe". But when we truly believe, we act in a similar way to the prospective visit from a loved one. We prepare for the arrival and our actions say "I believe".

Faith, could be translated into another five-letter word, that being Trust. Some, who don't understand your faith might prefer to call it folly. However, you are simply trusting your Daddy, that what He has promised is on the way, is really on the way and therefore you are acting accordingly.

We don't wait for our loved one to be ringing the doorbell or rattling the door knocker to believe they are coming. We took them at their word and are gaily waving our banner in the arrival's hall an hour before the flight is due to land.

In James if says faith without works is dead. So today let's take some steps that line up with what we believe. They might be just a couple of baby steps but they are steps nonetheless. When we truly believe, it is not going to rain, we don't carry an umbrella or a rain coat - we don't plan for the worst and when we truly believe Him, we act in a similar fashion.

When we trust Him for plan A, then we don't have a plan B, C and D. Have a blessed day. Take those steps and start ripping up plan Bs, Cs all the way to Z.

Proverbs 13v19

"A longing fulfilled is sweet to the soul"

Father thank You that my actions speak of trusting You and Your promises.

Burnt out – Reset

On a prayer walk with a friend we walked past the embers of two bonfires. Grey, charcoal showed what had been, but was no more. No warmth, nor heat and no capacity to light other fires.

The warning light on the dashboard comes on, so we pull off road and refill the empty tank so the vehicle can keep moving. Our stomachs grumble and growl we fill them and recharge the energy levels.

In other areas of our lives at times the warning light is flashing. Irritability, crankiness, fretful, low mood, poor concentration, lack of drive or motivation and where the flames of hope once licked now an air of heaviness pervades.

Matthew 11v28-30

"Come to me, all you who are weary and burdened and I will give you rest. Take my yoke upon you and learn from me for I am gentle and humble in heart and you will find rest for your souls. For my yoke is easy and my burden is light"

Worries, fears, regrets, guilt, anxieties, disappointments, problems, troubles, difficulties can at times appear overwhelming and fill our minds so there seems little room for anything else. Yet He invites us to come to Him when we are feeling weary, come to Him when we are overburdened and He will give us rest for our souls.

How many people would love rest from a racing mind? Who would like stress and fear to be replaced by His supernatural peace? For some even when they lay down sleep refuses to come. Yet He promises to give His beloved sleep.

Psalm 127v2

"For so he gives his beloved sleep"

Father thank You that we can come to You when we are feeling weary and burdened. We can lay down our burdens and cast our cares on You. We can be refreshed and refilled. Help me to come.

A *world without colour* – The oil of joy

We live in a time where most households boast multiple screens. It's hard for young people to fathom that their parents grew up without screens in their hands and their grandparents without them in their homes. In addition, many homes wouldn't have had the electricity to charge the handheld devices or to plug the televisions into when their grandparents were young. Then black and white television arrived to this nation. We watch nostalgically, movies made in black and white. However further progress was made and colour television arrived in Ireland in the 1970s. Some people today may feel like their life button is stuck on the black and white setting. There's no colour and no sparkle to how they are thinking or feeling.

Isaiah 61v3

"To appoint unto them that mourn in Zion, to give unto them beauty for ashes, the oil of joy for mourning, the garment of praise for the spirit of heaviness"

Most of us haven't a problem ringing a friend for prayer if unwell physically. However, on days when a spirit of heaviness clings making one feel like they're looking through a grey lens at life, we may be more reluctant to pick up the phone or tap out an email. The enemy whispers "you're a Christian; aren't you meant to be full of joy?" God has anointed other Christians to help us when feeling the blues, when a spirit of heaviness tries to blow in like the mist in the West of Ireland and settle putting a grey hue on everything.

Isaiah 61v1

"The spirit of the Lord God is upon me because the Lord hath anointed me to preach good tidings unto the meek, he hath sent me to bind up the broken-hearted, to proclaim liberty to the captives and the opening of the prison to them that are bound"

The NIV says "the release from darkness to the captives". Father help us to reach out for help when feeling the blues.

Father, I pray for anyone reading this today who feels like their setting is stuck on black and white, everything looks monochrome. I pray that You will give them beauty for ashes, that You will give them the oil of joy for mourning and in place of a spirit of heaviness You will give them a garment of praise. Father I thank You for this great exchange, in Jesus' name.

Leaving an imprint – Imprint

The dog delighted to make snow angels or more appropriately frost angels on the grass. I declined to join in her fun. Her imprint remained on the frosty grass long after we had proceeded with our walk. Like tyre imprints on a soft surface which remain when the vehicle has driven off.

What "imprints" will we leave today on those whose lives we rub against? Those we know and strangers whose path we cross today?

The boxer dog, left her imprint on Lily's snout after a quick hello greeting as they passed on the street. It can still be seen a week later. Tempted as one may be to snap or snarl at those they come into contact with even briefly. There is a better way, a higher path. As children of God, we are made in our heavenly Fathers image.

Genesis 1v27

"So, God created man in his own image, in the image of God he created them"

We are called to leave His imprint on the lives of those around us. When we chose the path of integrity even when others try and encourage us to do otherwise. When we chose to say no to temptation. When we make a choice to give a soft answer and not retaliate.

Proverbs 15v1

"A gentle answer turns away wrath but a harsh word stirs up anger"

When our choice is to carry love rather than a judgement stick for those around us. When we chose to forgive, even an offender who hasn't apologized and may never do so. When we chose to not be a grumbler and complainer even when there may be much more things to complain about than to rejoice about. When we choose to not engage in gossip. When we serve the needs of those around us, tirelessly and without blowing our own trumpet. And sometimes for no gain or thanks other than knowing that we are doing it in the name of the Lord Jesus. Colossians 3v17. When we do any of the above, we are leaving His imprint on those around us today.

Father help me to leave Your imprint on those whose lives I come into contact with to-day.

Don't light it – Don't set a match to it

The fire lay set, waiting for a match to bring life to it when the weather merited it. Needing to burn some papers I carefully placed them on top of the coals, and hey presto they were gone while the fire still lay nicely set. I repeated the process a few days later but, in an instant, the whole fire had ignited. I racked my brain as to how I could put it out for who bar the dog was going to benefit from its warmth at 7am? A tiny flame from a discarded match can start a roaring uncontrollable forest fire. Sometimes a word carelessly spoken about someone or some establishment and before long a fire is raging. Fires leave a mess when they have burnt out or been extinguished. I can't imagine anyone finding charred remains of bushes appealing to look at nor the ashes left in a grate pleasant to sit beside.

We need to be careful that our idle words don't cause a fire to ignite. A half-truth or a story passed on, can have the same effect as throwing a match on dry land. The fire takes over, it can be hard to extinguish and it choses which direction to take - not the one who lit it. While the internet and social media have many merits, news that would have taken a long time to pass on in days past, can now at the click of a few buttons travel great distances to multiple recipients with no effort required. Thus, causing at times great destruction, heartache and shame.

Proverbs 11v9

"With their mouths the godless destroy their neighbours but through knowledge the righteous escape"

Proverbs 16v28

"A gossip separates close friends"

Proverbs 11v13

"A gossip betrays a confidence but a trustworthy person keeps a secret"

Gossip can burn up someone's or an establishments good reputation. It can burn the chord that unites people and it can burn away a person's confidence or their trust in others. Let us never be the one who throws the gossip match and if we hear it coming our way, let's choose to stomp it out and prevent it turning into a roaring, raging uncontrollable fire.

Father if I have engaged in gossip, I repent today. Help me to choose to not gossip and to remove myself from gossip, and if I need to put records straight, please help me to do so.

Looking after the temple – Temple of the Holy Spirit

What if someone owned a car with a powerful engine, capable of great things but the owner didn't bother to take care of the car which housed it? No matter what potential the engine has, it's not going anywhere if the tyres are allowed to become threadbare and blow out. If the car is involved in an accident and there is major damage to the body of the car, even if the engine is unaffected by the crash, that car may still be considered a wreck or a write off.

1 Corinthians 6v19&20

"Or do you not know that your body is the temple of the Holy Spirit who is in you, whom you have from God, and you are not your own? You were bought at a price. Therefore, honour God with your bodies".

This verse tells us that our bodies are the temple of the Holy Spirit. Like the car owner who has the responsibility for not just taking care of what's under the bonnet but must tend to the complete car. We are each responsible for maintaining our "temples" of the Holy Spirit. For some people, exercise comes naturally, they embrace it, enjoy it and look forward to it. For others it is considered more of a necessity or a chore, while for some it doesn't even feature on their "to do list." Certain folks don't find it difficult to make healthy food choices but for others it takes greater effort. Any athlete knows that just as important as their training regimes are their times of rest. No life can be led with the speed dial at maximum, for an extended period of time without running the risk of burnout. Sprinters run fast but only over short distances, marathon runners, run slower but over much longer distances and they know how to pace themselves for every kilometre, so that they make it to the finish line. No matter how old or how young we are, we all need to take proper care of our temples, by taking adequate rest, by making good choices about what we will eat and drink and by ensuring we take exercise.

Romans 12v1

"Therefore, I urge you, brothers and sisters, in view of Gods mercy, to offer your bodies as a living sacrifice, holy and pleasing to God – this is your true and proper worship"

Father, You know each one of us, You know what we find easy and what areas we struggle in. Help us to make good choices in the care of our "temples", and while we may have failed in the past in this area, help us to remember that though a righteous man falls seven times he gets up.

Running water - Thankful

How many of us say a prayer of thanks every time we turn on a tap? Grateful for the fact that we don't have to draw water from a well or collect it from a stream. A couple of weeks ago, due to a burst pipe in the area, no running was coming into the house and the attic tank emptied quickly. I never realized the level of our daily water usage until I was driving to find a shop which still had bottled water in stock. Empty bottles were filled for us by a relative and more containers were filled from a Kildare County council tanker. In addition, I had taken for granted the amount of time and effort having running water saves.

When the problem was fixed the following day and water flowed from my taps. I said a prayer of thanks. I, like so many others take it for granted. If we stop and think there are many things in our lives that we take for granted and so many people in different facets of our lives who we can take for granted too. Unfortunately, so often it is not until something is not there or someone has gone from our lives, that we realize their true value.

Colossians 4v2

"Devote yourselves to prayer, being watchful and thankful"

Another version talks of having an attitude of thanksgiving. Complaining can become a habit, murmuring and grumbling can become a lifestyle. There are people who are pros at it and complain about everything from the government to their boss, the weather to their family and on and on and on they roll.

Let's be known as people who are thankful. Let's develop the habit of taking time to thank Him for the things and the people in our lives that we perhaps take for granted as they are always there like running water in our homes.

1 Thessalonians 5v16-18

"Rejoice always, pray continually, give thanks in all circumstances, for this is Gods will for you in Christ Jesus"

Let's make a point on a daily basis no matter which way the wind may be blowing to give thanks for the many blessings in our lives.

Father thank You. I am grateful for all You have blessed me with.

Refuge – Unexpected storms

Today there are many ways to learn about the weather other than holding a licked finger up outdoors to see what way the winds are blowing. I have a friend who helped keep "weather dial" in business with her phone calls.

No longer do those, whose livelihoods are weather dependent, like farmers and fishermen have to wait anxiously for the weather forecasts to be broadcast over the airwaves. They have instant, access to weather updates online.

In the days before all these weather alerts. People could get caught "off guard" by the arrival of a sudden storm. Rather than battling through the elements. They needed to seek shelter until the storm passed.

Some people have been caught off guard by the arrival of an unexpected storm in their lives. An unexpected redundancy, unfavourable test results from the doctor, an argument that blew across a good relationship suddenly, which has left a strain in its wake.

No matter what storm we may be facing. No matter its' intensity and regardless of if it wasn't forecasted or foreseen. We can take refuge in Him, until the storm has passed or blown over.

Psalm 46v1

"God is our refuge and our strength, an ever-present help in times of trouble"

He is not "ill prepared" and caught off guard by the "suddenlys" that blow or crash into our lives. He is not ill equipped for the storms that not only try and take the wind from our sails but that whisper, this will be the end of your mast "no more sailing".

Psalm 92v2

"I will say of the Lord "He is my refuge and my fortress. My God in whom I trust"

We are grateful for His refuge today from any storm that may be battering against the windowpanes of our life.

Father thank you that You are my refuge and my fortress. You haven't been caught off guard by any storm I have found myself in and You are my ever-present help in time of trouble.

The three Ps - Passion, Purpose, Perseverance

I love walking. Two of my children have failed to win me over to their love of running. I sat in traffic, amazed by how much ground was covered by a passing runner in a short period of time. It made me consider the race we are all running.

Each of us is called to run with PASSION the race set before us.

I Corinthians 9v24

"Do you not know that in a race all the runners run but only one gets the prize. Run in such a way as to get the prize"

Has your walking companion ever been a small child who doesn't want to walk? They move at a snail's pace dragging their heels behind them. More energy is exerted moving their mouths, complaining and whining than moving their feet. Some of us may relate to that child, maybe we have been dragging our heels and now it's time to increase the momentum and start running with passion.

We are called to run with PURPOSE.

Hebrews 12v1 talks about the race set out before us. A runner in a long-distance race, knows in which direction he is headed. He has an end goal and will have studied the race course. We need not only to have an end goal but also have to stay on course. My dog, off lead, never walks in a straight line. She is very distractible, will take multiple diversions and her journey ends up much longer than mine.

I Corinthians 9v26

"I do not run like someone running aimlessly. I do not fight like a boxer beating the air"

We are not to run aimlessly the race of life, but rather with purpose knowing that a crown awaits us.

1 Corinthians 9v25

"Everyone who competes in games goes into strict training. They do it to get a crown that will not last, but we do it to get a crown that will last forever"

The three Ps - Passion, Purpose, Perseverance

Run with PERSEVERANCE.

I have never run a marathon and don't plan to, but I have been around marathon runners in training. It takes perseverance to not quit and to make it all the way to the finish line. Many things along the 42km course could try and prevent them crossing the finish line. But they have a goal that they are determined to reach and they persevere.

Hebrews 12v1

"Let us run with perseverance the race marked out for us"

We have a promise in Isaiah 40v31 that we will run and not grow weary. If you are feeling weary today, physically or mentally remember what proceeds this portion of scripture.

Isaiah 40v31

"But they that wait upon the Lord shall renew their strength. They shall mount up with wings as eagles"

If we are feeling weary today, we can spend time waiting upon Him and let Him renew our strength.

Father help each of us today to run our race with Purpose, Passion and Perseverance. Those who have drifted from the course, lead them back on track. For those who are sluggish, help them to increase their speed and those who are weary, refresh them today please.

Dream

Father I thank you today for the dreams you have planted in each of our hearts. Some, have a thick layer of dust on them. For those for whom who that is the case Father help us to put on dust masks, pick up the feather dusters and get cleaning.

Others are lying right at the bottom of the "to do" tray. They keep being pushed there by the pressing things in our lives whose voices cry loudly "now" or "urgent". There have been times we have said, today is the day but the issues of life have deemed it not to be so. So, the dream has been put on the long finger and for some that finger has grown steadily longer with the passing months, years and even decades. The enemy whispers, "the dream has passed its sell by date".

Other dreams, sit on our desk with a sticky note on top "Disappointed". You see these are dreams out of our control which are yet to be answered prayers so we have given up on them and stopped praying with fervency about them. Today, He may be saying "dream again". "Trust again". "Pray again".

For some the dream tray lies empty and for different reasons. Dreams have already been accomplished or voices have said "you could never" or "that will never happen" or "you are too shy" or "finances would never permit it", "age rules me out", "family circumstances won't allow it" and on and on thc list goes, so you failed to dream. Father, please start to fill those empty dream trays today.

Now all dreams have to be put through the litmus test to see if they come from a pure heart. Once passed, we are free to dream.

Father thank You that this year will be the year for dreams moving from the "waiting to be delivered" ward through the delivery suite and into the post-natal ward. Father, You promise that as we delight ourselves in You that You will give us the desires of our heart. Father we thank You for many dreams becoming a reality.

Frozen over - Relationships

Our dog loves to find a puddle on a cold morning, that is frozen over. She charges into it, cracks the ice with her paw and then eats it. When I was a student, I did an Erasmus exchange in Belgium. For the first time I experienced a frozen lake. Now we students, were more careful than my dog and carefully tested the ice with one foot and then the other to check if it could take our weight. When happy it would, we stuck close to the edge first before venturing out into the middle of the lake. The heat of Spring arrived and melted our ice ring.

Perhaps someone reading this is faced with, not a frozen puddle to crack, nor lake to skate on, but a relationship that has gone cold. Maybe it was a gradual occurrence, it went frosty, then icy, before completely freezing over. Or perhaps it was a suddenly, an event or a miscommunication that caused the relationship to instantly freeze over.

Your heart longs to be back in fellowship. Sometimes we can be waiting for the other party to make the first move or to take the first step.

Romans 5v8

"But God shows His love for us, in that while we were still sinners, Christ died for us"

God loved first. God made the first move. Like the heat of Spring melted the frozen lake, let us trust, that the love of God that has been shed abroad in our hearts by the Holy Ghost, flowing through us, will start melting the ice thus causing the frozen relationship to thaw out.

1 John 4v9-11

"In this the love of God was made manifest among us, that God sent his only son into the world so that we might live through him. In this is love, not that we have loved God but that he loved and sent his son to be the propitiation for our sins. Beloved if God loved us, we also ought to love one another"

1 John 4v7

"Beloved, let us love one another, for love is from God"

Father, I pray for any relationship that has gone frosty, cold or completely frozen over. Help us to take the first step, to make the first move and to trust that Your love flowing through us will start to melt the ice in the relationship, in Jesus' name we pray. May there be reconciliation.

Next chapter – Moving on

I loved watching "This is your life" in my younger years presented by Eamon Andrews. He would turn the pages of a big book he held, and talk about different chapters in a person's life. As he did so, people stepped out from previous chapters of a person's life and into the studio. The programme was full of surprises and packed with emotion. At the end of the show the guest was presented with the book as the host declared "this is your life".

There are many things written in each of our "books of life". Highlights, accomplishments, achievements, people, milestones and of course other things we would erase if that was possible. Sadness, loss, mistakes and regret to name a few.

In each of our books, there are pages which are still blank, chapters yet to be written. For some today, I believe God is saying, it is time to turn the page. It's time to start writing the next chapter.

Jeremiah 29v11

"For I know the plans I have for you declares the Lord. Plans to prosper you and not to hurt you, to give you hope and a future"

The architect draws up the plans for the new build or extension. But they remain mere plans until the builder starts bringing them to pass. Some of us need to start digging foundations for our next chapter. Some need to start laying blocks and building walls.

While we can look back at old chapters of our life and reread them. We can never go back into these already written chapters just forward into the ones still to be written. We thank God for the next chapter in each of our lives and may we turn the page with excitement and anticipation

Father thank You for the already written chapters in my book of life. Show me please when it is time to turn the page and start a new chapter.

Beak off – John 10v10

I watched out the kitchen window, the dog jumping from the trampoline, tearing across the decking and leaping high into the air. She is normally a very friendly dog who wants to greet every dog we pass and has been known to throw herself at the feet of random strangers.

This was different. She had a beautiful, smelling fresh bone and a magpie had the audacity to think he could take a look or have a peck at it. Beak off was the message he received.

John 10v10

"The thief comes only to steal and kill and destroy; I have come that they may have life, and have it to the full"

John 10v10 states that the thief comes to rob, kill and destroy. Sometimes pilfering has gone on for such a long time in areas of our life, that we become almost accustomed to it. The magpie returned for a second attempt but was reminded again, no trespassing.

At times we need to be like my Lily; rise up in our God given authority and protect what is ours to protect. We need to do some running leaps, declaring hands off my health, leave my marriage alone, my children are out of bounds, don't touch my finances, leave my mental wellbeing alone, stop messing with my relationships and the list could go on and on.

The message is simple to the enemy. No trespassing on our property today. No stealing and no robbing and I love the verse in Proverbs 6 where it says if the thief is caught, he must restore seven-fold.

Proverbs 6v31

"And thieves who get caught must pay back seven times what was stolen and lose everything"

We claim seven-fold restoration for the areas that we have been robbed in. We erect no trespassing signs on the perimeters of our lives and if an intruder gets in like the magpie to our garden - we do like my Lily and boldly run him.

Have a blessed day!

Boundaries – Erecting boundaries

The flimsy timber fence had been pulled down, the shrubs dug up and a stone wall built in their place. The family pet couldn't escape through it and a high wind wouldn't cause it to topple. A toddler doesn't understand boundaries - and will happily wander over to join in someone else's picnic without an invitation. Our dog, if let, would follow a scent into a stranger's garden uninvited and in through someone's front door. The toddler will be taught boundaries, I am not so sure about the dog. If new boundaries get erected, they can initially cause irritation or upset. Your neighbour liked wandering in through a hole in the hedge to pick a few herbs to garnish their dinner with and now they can't because a wall stands where once a hedge did.

When we were growing up, we were taught what were "polite" hours of the day to make a phone call. In this era of 24/7 communication, my own children look at me blankly when I try and explain "office hours" and that there is not someone permanently sitting in certain businesses ready to answer their calls.

Boundaries are good. However, if there have never been any, offense may try and creep in when a cement mixer arrives and building on the boundary wall starts. So too in relationships that have had no boundaries, when some are tried to be established - they can cause upset. However, that is not reason for tearing down the new wall nor a reason to let people have free roam and free access to our lives in a way that we are uncomfortable with.

It is better to have boundaries than to have none and to be doing things "grudgingly and of necessity". Having boundaries doesn't mean we aren't "walking in love". Jesus took himself away from the crowd to rest and pray. If the wall didn't replace the hedge between the neighbours, the herb bushes would be stripped bare and nothing left for the family that resided there. Similarly, if there are relationships that lack boundaries, one can sometimes be left feeling depleted of their time, resources and energy.

A boundary wall is not a "no entry". Rather in each new wall, a door can be put that can be opened and closed and the guest invited in through.

Father if there are areas of my life that I need to erect some boundaries in, help me to do so without causing offense. If the shoe is on the other foot and someone has erected some boundaries on me, help me to approach the situation with understanding and please protect my heart from offense.

Use the Clutch – **Slow down**

I was the first of us five children to be taught to drive. Some things were so obvious to the instructor, my mother that she either didn't remember or feel it necessary to tell me. So, the car made embarrassing noises each gear change as my foot was still firmly lodged on the accelerator. Approaching a junction at speed on one occasion. she told me to use the clutch to slow the car down. "How?" I asked as that would involve crossing my legs. She had overlooked to teach me which pedal was used by which foot.

There are times we need to use the clutch to slow the car down. If we don't, the emergency stop method of slamming on the brakes might be necessary further down the road. It's better to slow down by using the clutch than to have to bring the car to an emergency stop. It's easier to keep the car in motion at a slower pace than to have to stop completely and have to restart the engine. I believe God has been whispering to some, use your clutch and slow down. When we do this no emergency braking will be required further down the line. Road signs warn of what lies ahead, what's around the corner and many imply the need to slow down. Go down a gear. Slow the car down. Jesus took time away from the crowds and from the needs of the people to rest and talk to His Father.

Mark 4v35,38

"That day when evening came, He said to His disciples "Let us go over to the other side" Leaving the crowd behind they took Him along........v 38 Jesus was in the stern sleeping on a cushion".

Jesus wasn't stressing over the needs of those who they had left on the shore, He wasn't fretting wondering if they were offended that He needed some time, rather He was sleeping. In Matthew 14, we read of Jesus ministering and healing the sick, we read of His compassion for the people, we read how He performed miracles, walked on water and multiplied bread and fish. However, in verse 23 we also read how He went up onto a mountainside after He dismissed the crowd, by Himself and prayed. If Jesus needed times to physically rest and if He needed times away from the crowd to connect with His Heavenly Father, then how much more do we? I believe He is saying to some, use the gear stick, slow down the pace you are traveling at. Come aside from the crowd and their needs, rest and connect with your Heavenly Father.

Father help me to know when it is time to slow down and be refreshed and recharged.

Separated – Holiness

Much of what I was taught in secondary school has long vanished from memory. However, I vividly recall being taught in home economics the art of meringue making. The trick lay in having beautifully beaten egg whites. Before the beater could get to work turning our liquid whites into thick peaks, there were steps to be rigidly followed. These read more like an avoidance list. If water was in the bowl or the tiniest piece of shell or if egg yolk slid into the bowl alongside the precious egg whites, our beautiful meringues were doomed. The egg white needed to be perfectly separated from the egg yolk in order to guarantee success. I still think of that teacher, when I am separating eggs for a roulade to-day.

2 Corinthians 6v17

"Come out from them and be separate says the Lord. Touch no unclean thing and I will receive you"

What does that verse mean for the Christian, does it mean we're to live in a bubble, only interacting with other bubble living Christians? How will we impact this world if we cut ourselves off from it? We are called to love the unsaved, to pray for them, to reach out to them. But loving a person doesn't mean we condone all their actions. We don't join in activities that we know are wrong to make them feel at ease nor do we swallow the lie, that to reach them we need to be "doing what they are doing".

Ephesians 5v11

"Have no fellowship with the unfruitful works of darkness"

We are not called to "fit in", in the world we live in, even though doing so would often guarantee an easier life. Just like the meringue mixture wouldn't work unless the two parts of the egg were completely separated, we can't be fooled into thinking "well what harm"? What harm, if I do what all around me seem to be doing? What harm to put a little bit of egg yolk into the mixing bowl when there is so much white in it? What harm will a little bit of sin do when so much of how I live my life is pleasing to my heavenly Father?

1 Peter 1v16 says "be holy because I am holy". We are not to try and simply "act" holy but we are to "be" holy and from that position our actions, attitudes and standards will flow. What pleases Him will please us and what displeases Him will be displeasing to us. We will keep loving the sinner but won't put ourselves in situations that the sin itself starts rubbing off on us like the rotten apple in the bottom of the fruit bowl which starts to turn the other apples around it brown.

It's Not Over – He is not finished

The lyrics of the song playing on Spirit radio grabbed my attention. "It's not over". At times we drive a new route and what we perceive as a way forward leads us to a dead end. We have driven into a cul-de-sac.

At times, in different situations and scenarios it can feel like we are looking at a dead end. We have reached the end of the road, there appears to be no way forward in the marriage, no more road for the dream, all hope is gone for the relationship, the exam result says it is over, the ministry seems to have run out of ground, the thing we have prayed and trusted and believed for appears to now be an impossibility.

Yet He says "it's not over". He is not finished.

He says I know the plans I have for you, plans to prosper you and not to hurt you to give you hope and a future. It's not over. Things might not have worked out as we planned or hoped but He says "it is not over" He has a plan, He has a way out of the dead-end situation, He has a way forward and we need simply to trust Him.

Isaiah 55v8

"For My thoughts are not your thoughts, nor are your ways my ways," says the LORD."

Just because we don't know the way doesn't mean there's not a way. As the words of that song encouraged me this morning, I pray they bring you encouragement wherever you are today and whatever situation you find yourself in.

"It's not over"

Father when it feels like I have driven into a cul-de-sac and met a dead end and can see no way forward, help me to look to You, for strength, encouragement and direction.

Look Up – Look to Him

Walking on an unlit path a couple of years ago, I suddenly found myself heading towards the ground. I had tripped over the dog. When one falls over there is nothing much to see before our eyes. However, there is plenty one could feel - physical pain, embarrassment, annoyance or shame.

Small children have on occasions been known to throw themselves on the ground by choice, where they unashamedly vent their emotions. Sometimes, one finds themselves lying on the ground, helped there by the push of another's hand or tripped up on purpose by an outstretched leg of another.

While physically still standing we can at times feel like we have fallen over - pushed to the ground by another's actions, tripped up by our own stumbling or thrown there by self out of sheer frustration. All we can see around us is dirt and dust.

Sometimes it is simply a matter of rolling over and seeing things from a different angle.

Psalm 121v1

"I will lift up my eyes to the hills. Where does my help come from? My help comes from the Lord"

Our help comes from the Lord. The above verse puts the onus on us to look up, even when we may feel low, downtrodden, lonely or disappointed. We are to look up. When lying face down, one can't see the outstretched hand that is ready to pull us back to our feet.

Psalm 46v1

"God is our refuge and strength, a very present help in time of trouble".

No matter what situation we find ourselves in today or what emotions are raging in our soul. We can choose to do as the scripture says and stop looking downward but rather, look up towards the outstretched hand of our Heavenly helper. We trust Him and thank Him for His help wherever we may need it today.

Father I choose to look up today, I will lift up my eyes to the hills for my help comes from the Lord.

DADDY – He is our Daddy

I sat with two friends and chatted. One talked about her father. She always refers to him as "Daddy" and talks with such fondness and love. As I listen, I don't see an 80-year-old lady but a little girl who is bursting with love and admiration for her Daddy.

No matter if we are the tender age of eight, the more mature age of eighty or lie somewhere in between, our Heavenly Father is our Daddy. Not a distant, absentee, judgemental, hard man. But rather a loving Daddy who we can trust to never fail us, whose arms we can run into when we hurt physically or have been wounded by the words or actions of another. When facing complex situations that we can't figure out an answer to, or if battling mental turmoil, addiction, depression or fatigue, we can look to our Daddy. He will never leave us and never let us down. For He is our Abba Father.

Romans 8v15

"For you did not receive the spirit of bondage again to fear, but you received the spirit of adoption by whom we cry out "Abba Father"

Galatians 4v6

"And because you are sons, God has sent forth the spirit of His Son into your hearts, crying out Abba Father"

Today let's be like my friend Gwen and have childlike trust and dependence in our heavenly Daddy.

Matthew 18v2 & 3

"He called a little child to him and placed the child among them. Truly I tell you unless you change and become like little children, you will never enter the kingdom of heaven"

Father help me to see you as my Daddy. Where my image of You has been warped by earthly Fathers, please heal me, in Jesus' name I pray.

The Sea – Stay spiritually alert

I inherited my mother's love of the sea. She loved walking beside it, picnicking on the sand and was known to swim in all seasons in the Irish Sea. Despite enjoying its great beauty, she instilled in her children a healthy respect for it. I quote her sea rules to her grandchildren.

Standing on the shore the crystal clear, gentle waters lapping around their ankles the bathers may be beckoned to deeper waters but unseen from the beach is the under currents and the rip tides that once caught in are very hard to escape from.

When a commercial fisherman is preparing to head out for a few days at sea he doesn't stand in the garden lick his finger and find the wind direction. He listens attentively to the forecast to see what is coming down the line. A special sea area forecast is broadcast on our national broadcaster.

We need to stay spiritually alert; Jesus asked his disciples to keep watch in the garden of Gethsemane and yet three times he found them sleeping on the job. He knew what lay ahead.

When all around us is calm and glistening it's not time to take to the hammock, for a snooze. Our adversary the devil prowls around and what better prey to find than a sleeping Christian.

1 Peter 5v8

"Be alert and of sober mind. Your enemy the devil prowls around like a roaring lion looking for someone to devour"

What an easy catch for a lion in the wild to find some sleeping prey. Let's not be caught off guard and sleeping by our enemy.

Like the fisherman who turns the radio dial to tune into the long-term forecast. We need to stay spiritually alert, with the dial tuned in to what is being transmitted from heaven.

The command to pray without ceasing is as much for calm days as for when a storm is brewing or in full force.

So, let's all check our dials today.

Left behind – Don't give up!

Have you ever sat frustrated in traffic watching time tick by only to arrive at the airport, to discover your flight has already departed? Have you rushed through crowded streets reaching the station to watch your train pulling away from the platform? Perhaps you were tempted to dive in and chase the ferry that was chugging out of the harbour as you stood watching from the quayside?

Has the enemy ever whispered in your ear or roared loudly in both ears "you have missed the boat?" Time has not gone in your favour, in fact time has run out. The healing flight has just taken to the air while you're left standing at the departure gate. The marriage train is puffing to the next station while you remain alone on the platform. The promotion ship has sailed and you are scratching your head on the harbour wall, knowing you were the most qualified candidate.

A wise friend said to me a few months back regarding our offspring "what's for them won't pass them by". The same can be said for each of us. Even if it feels like we have been left behind on the station platform, at the harbour wall, bus stop or the airport departure gate, we can keep trusting God that what is for us won't pass us by. The passing of time is not a message from heaven declaring "it won't happen" but rather simply the passing of time.

Yes, that unsaved loved one you have worn many trouser knees out praying for, can still come to know Jesus as their Saviour. The family situation that appears unsolvable can be resolved. That ache in your body can be healed and the darkness and despair you wake to each morning can lift like a morning mist and not return. So rather than focusing on what has already departed, instead we can get out the timetable and see when the next bus, train, ferry of flight is due heading to our required destination and be ready to climb on board.

Galatians 6v9

"Let us not become weary in doing good, for at the proper time we will reap a harvest if we don't give up"

There lies the key, in not giving up. You may have watched multiple flights leave without you. Many buses may have arrived at your bus stop full to capacity so you weren't allowed on but don't grow weary and don't give up, you will not be left behind.

Father help me not to give up and not to quit.

Fear not – **Don't fear**

When fear comes knocking at the door of your mind, it can feel like a physical uninvited and unwanted visitor ringing on your front door late at night leaving you quaking and shaking. We have all heard or maybe even used the expressions "fear gripped my heart" or "I was paralysed with fear". Fear of so many things - fear of tomorrow, fear of what the doctor might say, fear of lack, fear of calamity, fear of being alone, and the list could go on and on. Multiple times, in the Bible we read the words "Fear not". In fact, 80 times we are told and commanded not to fear.

Isaiah 35v4

"Say to those with fearful hearts "Be strong, do not fear your God will come"

Timothy tells us that God has not given us a spirit of fear but of power, of love and a sound mind. Fear does not come from our loving, faithful Heavenly Father.

For many it is a struggle to "not fear" to others it seems a complete impossibility. When the pile of white unopened envelopes gets steadily higher, when the exam dates draw closer, when the future looks uncertain, when bad news is blaring over the airwaves. Fear can come knocking and ringing loudly and persistently on the door of your mind. The unseen force, demanding to be let in.

Psalm 34v4

"I sought the Lord and He answered me and delivered me from all my fears"

I find this scripture both encouraging but also liberating. Because many have tried with all their might to not let fear in but despite their good intentions and best efforts, fear made it in. It crashed through every barrier; it broke every lock. The good news for those who feel completely hopeless and at a loss as to how to get it out is found in Psalm 34v4. Seek Him and trust Him to deliver you from every fear. Don't be overwhelmed by the fear but put your efforts into seeking Him and let Him set you free from fear.

Father I pray for those reading this who are overwhelmed with fear and feel helpless against it. Father you say, You have not given us a spirit of fear but of power, love and a sound mind, so we know that fear does not come from You. As they seek You, please deliver them from their fears.

Let me in! – God's direction

You stand peering in the glass door of the establishment. There are people inside and yet all your efforts to enter have been in vain. You push against the door even harder this time as you check the opening times written on the door. But the door doesn't give way and you remain outside looking in.

Suddenly your eyes are drawn to four little black letters which when put together hold the key to your issue. For all your great efforts have been in vain and a waste when all that was needed was to simply "pull" the door towards you instead of "pushing" it from you.

Sometimes we are faced with a situation that we have tried in vain to resolve. We have prayed and prayed about it and yet we feel like that person looking through the closed glass door. And yet maybe there is a simple solution, maybe rather than following our head we need to listen to our heart and change the way we have been broaching the issue and therein lies the solution.

John 10v27

"My sheep hear my voice and follow me"

Listening to and following His direction even in the small everyday things can often save a lot of wasted effort and exertion. It is not always an audible voice that we will hear but the still small voice leading and directing us.

Isaiah 30v21

"And your ears shall hear a voice behind you saying, this is the way walk in it"

And when we hear that voice and reasoning tries loudly to shout it down and then the voice of logic screams even louder, we need to silence those voices and do what we know what He is leading us to do and all the frustration from standing pushing the door will fall away when a simple pull opens it and we have gained entry.

Thank You, Heavenly Father, for Your leading and guiding this day. Thank You for the voice behind me saying this is the way, walk in it.

Take a moment - Creation

When we look through a magnifying glass, we are not changing the size of what we are looking at but rather our ability to see it.

Psalm 34v3

"O magnify the Lord with me and let us exalt his name together"

It's hard to fathom for even the brightest of human minds or to put into words the size of the God we serve. Yet sometimes situations, problems, issues and just daily life can become so big, filling every corner of our thoughts, that He is almost squashed out. We may need to take a step back and spend time magnifying the Lord.

Psalm 8v3,4

"When I look at your heavens, the work of your fingers, the moon and the stars which you have set in place, what is man that you are mindful of him and the son of man, that you care for him".

Sometimes we have to look no further than to His creation to be reminded of His greatness and to reflect on His faithfulness. If you are feeling bogged down today with commitments and a work load so long that you can't see to the end of it, if your heart is heavy, as the airwaves are so full of tragic news or if you yourself have situations that are pressing on you trying to take hold of your emotions. Then can I suggest that you simply "take a moment".

Take a moment to enjoy His creation and be reminded of the magnitude of the God we serve. Observe the beauty of the trees, look at the patterns in the clouds above you, watch the waves roll up the sand, look at the steadfastness of the hills, listen to the birdsong, and on and on the list could go.

Psalm 121v1,2

"I lift up my eyes to the mountains, where does my help come from? My help comes from the Lord, the maker of heaven and earth"

Father help me to see You in the creation around me today.

Store up! – Store up in the good times

On a wet, cold Winters morning, some of us may wish we could hibernate like the bears. While squirrels don't hibernate, they choose to avoid the cold by staying in their dens until brighter weather returns.

Now of course it wouldn't take long until we would be forced to venture outdoors because unlike the bears, we aren't able to eat plenty in one season to carry us through the next. Nor do most of us have three years of food squirreled away, for this is what the squirrels do each Summer and Autumn.

However, we can apply some of their wisdom. Bears eat and drink practically nonstop during the Autumn months to prepare for their time in hibernation. Which of us, at some time, has not felt the cold winds of adversity blowing against our health or relationships or an icy downpour drenching our finances or a storm brewing someplace else in our lives?

We don't want to be forced out in the elements in search of a word or a promise for our situation when we can simply go to the store cupboard of our hearts and meditate on what we have already put there when the sun was shining, the weather warm and no cold breeze blowing.

Deuteronomy 11v18

"You shall lay up these words of mine in your heart and in your soul"

Psalm 119v11

"Your word, I have hidden in my heart"

Just like the squirrels who are busy in Autumn, when food is in plentiful supply and the weather milder. In seasons where there are no rain clouds overhead, or winds howling let us be diligent to store up His word in our hearts.

Proverbs 7v1,3

"My son keep my words and store up my commands within you....write them on the tablet of your heart"

Let us encourage today, the young people in our homes, families and churches to do likewise, to take the time to store God's word in their hearts, one scripture at a time, so that when the storms come, they are ready and prepared and have no need to go out in the elements.

131

Remember me for – **What are we made of?**

Benches in parks or overlooking the sea with small brass plaques. I stop and read the inscriptions and think of who they speak of. One short sentence, giving a glimpse into a stranger's life.

At a funeral service when the deceased is spoken of, there is rarely a reference to what model of car they drove, what brand of handbag hung on their arm or how many pairs of shoes graced their wardrobe. Rather they are remembered for their feats, accomplishments and of what "stuff" they were made. One of my children loves teddy bears, if all the stuffing was removed from each one what would be the heartbeat of each bear?

If our lives thus far could be summed up in a single sentence, how would it read? No two sentences would be the same, some may contain the word loyalty, others faithful, one may speak of diligence or perhaps kindness, determination or courageous may make it into your sentence. Perhaps yours would talk of bravery. There are many things it could say.

Then there is the sentence that only He could write about us, for there are things that only He has seen and heard, deeds done, prayers said when not convenient, giving that truly cost, forgiveness that was very hard to give for acts which never should have been committed, sacrifices made that only He knows the magnitude of, tears shed that only He saw.

He has seen for He sees and knows even if no one else knows or maybe ever will and we can take comfort from this. In the book of Acts we read – Cornelius' prayers and giving have come up as a memorial. When feeling unappreciated, when considering that what you do is never noticed, when feeling like quitting, remember, He has seen, He sees and will see.

Remember me thus....

Hands up – Does God hear me?

Have you ever stood before a group of children and asked for a volunteer to do something favourable or to be the recipient of something nice? Hands shoot up. You scan the sea of excited faces before you and your attention is drawn to the middle of the crowd. For standing there, is a little girl, hand raised as high as physically possible and for fear of being overlooked she is adding height to her stature by leaping in the air. Out of her mouth is coming one simple word, "Me". Which is on repeat.

Have you ever felt like that little girl in the midst of a large crowd? Your hand up as high as physically possible, you wave madly and shout, "Me, Me, what about me God?"

Sometimes it can feel like everyone around us is being picked ahead of us, their prayers are being answered. They are being blessed and giving testimony and the cry of our heart is "God, please don't forget my prayers, some which were first uttered a long time ago" or "God, did you hear when I spoke to you about a certain matter?"

Praise God, that no matter how big the crowd is, no matter how high those around us can raise their hands or how loud they are able to shout. He sees us, He hears us when we pray and He will bring answers. We will not be overlooked.

Psalm 31v6&8

"Be strong and courageous, do not be afraid or tremble for the Lord your God is the one who goes with you. He will not fail you or forsake you, the Lord is the one who goes ahead of you. He will be with you. He will not fail you or forsake you. Do not fear or be dismayed"

The above verses tell us four things not to do and two things to do – we are not to be afraid, but be strong, we are not to tremble but instead be courageous, don't fear and don't be dismayed. Why? The verse tells us four reasons why - He goes with us, He will not fail us, He will not forsake us and He goes ahead of us. I choose to personalise it – God, you will not forsake me, You are with me, You will not fail me, You are going ahead of me.

Father, for those whose arm is weary from waving and they are hoarse from shouting, please reassure them today that You are the great I am. You are what you said You are and You will do what You said you will do. You will not fail them. They are not forgotten; they won't be by passed.

Well, fix it dear Henry – Fixing tricky situations

As I started to think about what I was going to write a song from my youth started to play in my mind, the theme of which was in line with what I have been meditating on. "There's a hole in my bucket, dear Liza, dear Liza, a hole in my bucket dear Liza a hole. "Well fix it dear Henry, dear Henry, dear Henry, well fix it dear Henry." Does it ring a bell for anyone? The song goes on to discuss what is needed to be done to fix the bucket, which is no simple task.

Some reading this may be of the generation that when something was broken you fixed it, mended it or darned it. Others may be of a different generation, and when something is broken, worn or torn, the solution is to throw it out and get a replacement.

The second option while many times costlier often requires less time and much less effort. There is a time to throw away and there is a time to fix. Sometimes we want to run from a messy situation in our lives. A broken relationship, a strained friendship, a difficult situation at work or a church issue. There are times when that is the correct thing to do but on other occasions the opposite is the case. God is directing us not to give up on the family member, job, friend or church that we are having issues with. Rather He is calling us to get out the darning needle and thread it and to mend some holes. Or He wants us to get some plaster and a trowel and patch up a hole.

Sometimes a new pair of socks sounds much more appealing than an old pair with the heel darned in them. But just as many a sock can be salvaged and saved from the bin so too, we are not meant to give up and run from every hard, tricky or sticky situation that arises in our lives. We are called to be peacemakers, ones who rebuild rather than tear down. People who will build bridges rather than blow them up and ones who are always ready and willing to forgive even when we don't hear the word sorry.

Romans 12v18

"If possible, so far as it depends on you, be at peace with all men"

Hebrews 12v14

"Pursue peace with all men"

Father, please show me today if there are relationships that I am tempted to give up on, that You want me to try and make amends in.

Our shelter in the storm - **Our refuge**

As I approached the front door, my daughter said "listen to the storm". In our heated home, with fire lighting and dinner on the go, I had been blissfully unaware of what was happening outside of our haven. That was until we left the house and stepped outside. A few hundred meters from the house people were trying to saw a fallen tree that was blocking the road and when we got to our destination the storm was roaring at a great intensity. The wind howled and whistled through the trees, signs were rattling, and you were very aware of the strength of the storm. If you had to give it an emotion, you would say red roaring angry.

Thank God, in the storms of life that we face we have a haven to take refuge and shelter in.

Psalm 91v1&2

"Because we dwell in the secret place of the Most High, we shall abide under the shadow of the Almighty, we will say of the Lord, He is our refuge and our fortress, Our God in Him we will trust"

Psalm 46v1-3

"God is our refuge and strength, a very present help in trouble. Therefore, we will not fear, even though the earth be removed, and though the mountains be carried into the midst of the sea, though it's waters roar and be troubled, though the mountains shake with its swelling"

We can come in from the elements and take rest in Him and not be anxious but rather as it tells us in verse 10 of Psalm 46 "Be still and know that I am God".

Father thank You that You are my refuge from the storms of life, You are my strength and a very present help in trouble.

On your marks – Timing

Walking in the grounds of Castletown, on the path down by the river, one couldn't but fail to notice how high the river was. It looked ready to burst its banks and overflow. If only, some of the water could be released from the bursting river which looked so uncomfortable.

Some of us have heard Gods call, we know without a doubt what direction He is leading us in. Maybe it has been confirmed to us through prophetic words from others. As time passes, we can begin to feel like the river Liffey today and I am sure many other rivers across this nation after all the rain. The cry of our heart is "Release me Lord". We can even question "Lord, did I hear you say go, did you release me to step out and step into what you have for me to do?"

The athlete knows what race he will run in, he knows the distance he will run and the start time of his event. He goes to the start line and prepares, he hears on your marks, then set but he doesn't move until he hears the all-important word, which is Go. In our eagerness let's wait till that important word of release comes from on high. I have sat watching young athletes in national competitions approach the start line with a mixture of excitement and slight trepidation. They have trained hard; they have qualified to run in the nationals. They set their starting blocks and then the unthinkable happens, they move too soon before the starters gun. No one will cross the finish line in their lane for they have been disqualified and asked to leave the track.

One particular relay race sticks in my mind. I recognised the singlet being worn by the teenage girls. The reason I knew it was because they were good and I had seen them win in previous races and walk around proudly wearing their medals. They had great potential to do well in this final, they had done well in their heat. Unfortunately, they never got the chance to run because runner one went before the gun. She may have simply twitched in the blocks. It was just a simple mistake but a costly one that required much Kleenex. Let's determine in our excitement and in our enthusiasm to wait on Him to give the release, for He knows when we are ready and His timing is always perfect.

Psalm 31v15

"My times are in your hands"

So, if that is you, standing on the start line, you have heard on your marks, you have heard, get set. Well, keep listening GO will come.

Time for the brasso – Shine for Him

There was a brass letter box and door knob on our front door growing up. Due to all the handling and the oxygen in the air, they would lose their shine. The little tin of Brasso would be taken out, a dab poured on a cotton cloth and the brass rubbed to remove the tarnish and restore its' shine.

The sitting room side board and my mother's dressing table was where the silver sat. Sheets of old newspaper would be laid down, the dull looking silverware collected from around the house and placed on it. This time it was the Silvos' turn. A layer was applied to each piece of silverware, they would then be polished until their shine has been restored.

Some Christians can feel at times like the tarnished door knob or the dull silverware. Joy and excitement have been replaced by drudgery and obligation. Busyness, even doing good and noble things and attending to kingdom business can on occasions lead to burnout. Time spent recharging in His presence is essential. What we do in the kingdom needs to flow from our relationship with Him. To some of His children, He may be whispering "where are you for, I haven't heard from you recently?"

Matthew 5v14

"You are the light of the world. A city set on a hill cannot he hidden"

We are called to shine for Him. For some to get the mercury rising in the joy thermometer and the light shining, there are simple and practical steps that can be taken. Sometimes it is simply having the courage to do what we know in our hearts we need to do without being afraid of upsetting others. Sometimes to get that time with Him, it means saying "no" to other things around us.

Deuteronomy 41v6

"Be strong and courageous. Do not be afraid or terrified because of them, for the Lord your God goes with you, he will never leave you nor forsake you".

The badge - **Bravery**

Many a scout or guide uniform is decorated with badges earned through successfully completing different tasks. Many people wear an emblem, not visible to the naked eye but one with five little letters written on it, "Brave".

One earned their badge by courage shown when walking through challenging times with their health. Another earned theirs by being like one of the three young men, Shadrach, Meshach and Abednego, who would not bow to pressure to do something which they knew in their heart and soul to be wrong, despite what this stand could mean for them.

Hebrews 13v6

"The Lord is my helper; I will not be afraid. What will man do to me?"

It's a choice to not bow to pressure from boss, colleague, friend, neighbour or family member to do what we know to be wrong.

For some the badge was earned by trusting God and doing what He asked them to do even when it was something they could never do in their natural strength and with their natural ability. Like Moses or Gideon who didn't feel they had what it took to accomplish what God had asked them to do, but they obeyed.

Many times, in the Bible we read the words "Be strong and courageous" so no matter what we face today or in the days ahead. Let these words bring sweet comfort to our souls.

Psalm 27v14

"Be strong and let your heart take courage"

Some He led or may be leading to leave their home shores and family to go to another but He promises in Mark 10 that "no one who has left home or brothers or sisters or mother or father or children or fields for me and the gospel will fail to receive a hundred times as much in this present age: homes, brothers, sisters, mothers, children and fields".

Father no matter what I am facing today or in this season, help me to be brave.

Good intentions – God intentions

If our lives were a garden and a new addition was made for every "good intention" that never got fulfilled - what would our garden look like? Some would no doubt be worthy winners of the Chelsea flower show.

How often have we thought or said - "I meant to", to self or others? I meant to call you or visit you or text you or email you, I meant to give practical or financial help. I meant to, I meant to, I meant to......

Do you know some of those "good intentions" that we let slip by may be "God intentions"? Our phone call to someone or our encouraging card, our knock at their front door or our reaching out to someone may be an answer to their prayer or the cry of their heart.

Today let's be sensitive to His prompting and His leading and perhaps He will show us what "good intentions" that have been put on the very, very, long finger are His intentions.

1 Thessalonians 5v11

"Therefore encourage one another and build each other up"

There may be someone in our sphere of influence who is grappling with the deeper issues of life, questioning and searching and we hold the key and have the answer.

Maybe the "God intention" for that individual is for us to sow a seed or to water a seed that has already been sown by another and let God bring the increase.

I am grateful to the people who followed His leading and guiding and prayed for me or my family over the years. For those who reached out in love or kindness or in a practical manner. I am grateful for those who followed the "God intentions", and oft times were an answer to my prayers.

Father help us this day in the midst of all that is going on to be sensitive to Your promptings and Your leading so that when this day ends, we can have a sense of satisfaction knowing that we haven't added to our list of good intentions but have acted and moved some from the "to do" list to the "completed" section.

The record player – Speaking with wisdom

A record slipped onto the player of my heart. Needle moved into place and a simple children's song began to play in my head.

"Keep, your tongue from evil, keep your tongue. Keep your tongue from evil, keep your tongue and your lips from speaking lies". This song is based on Psalm 34v13

It is echoed in 1 Peter 3v10 "whoever would love life and see good days must keep their tongue from evil and their lips from deceitful speech". Which of us doesn't want to experience good days?

One doesn't have to rack their brains for long to consider what type of evil this verse may refer to - gossip, slander, perversion, unconstructive criticism, arguments, lies and the list goes on and on.

Let's determine to use our tongue this day not to tear down, belittle or cause pain or shame but in an opposing manner.

Proverbs 31 tells us that the virtuous woman speaks with wisdom and faithful instruction is on her tongue. We are also told in Proverbs if we guard our mouths and our tongues, we will keep ourselves from calamity.

Proverbs 15 refers to the soothing tongue, what a blessing to be able to soothe the wounded, hurting heart of a loved one or stranger with our words

Ephesians 4v10 says "do not let any unwholesome talk come out of your mouths, but only what is helpful for building others up...that it may benefit those who listen"

Father, please help us to use the tongues that you have given us today in constructive manners. Use us this day to bring soothing words to those who are in pain. Help us to speak words that will bring hope, where there is despair. Guide us when bringing instruction and giving advice. Father may we speak only truth, about You, about situations and about others. Where there is turmoil and unrest, enable us to speak peace. Let thanksgiving and praise and honour for You and all You have done for each one of us come out our lips this day.

Thank you, Father.

Silver Haired Wisdom – Wisdom from experience

He reached up with the garden shears to get the high bits way above his head. He had youth on his side so despite the great heat it was no bother to him. He also had strength and agility.

Beside him stood silver haired wisdom. She may not have done what he did physically with such ease but she was the voice of wisdom and knowledge, drawing from her well of experience.

Proverbs 20v29

"The glory of young men is their strength. And the honour of old men is their hair"

Job 12v12

"Is not wisdom found among the aged? Does not long life bring understanding?"

Young people are full - full of energy and passion, full of dreams and excitement and zeal. However, at times, they need the guidance of those who have walked the road ahead of them.

Proverbs 1v8&9

"Hear my son your father's instruction and forsake not your mothers teaching for they are a graceful garland for your neck and pendants for your hair"

Even while young these young people can be examples to those around them.

1 Timothy 4v12

"Let no one despise you for your youth, but set the believers an example in speech, in conduct, in love, in faith, in purity"

We thank God for the passion and zeal of youth and we thank Him for silver haired wisdom. We pray this day that each will be a blessing to the other.

The gift of the Day Ahead - Today

I watched the sun rise over the mountains yesterday morning. A promise of a fresh, new day. Last night I watched the same sun set over a different mountain. That day will never be lived again. As I write the sun is rising again, ushering in another brand new, never lived before day.

Psalm 113v3

"From the rising of the sun to its setting. The name of the Lord is to be praised"

Praise Him for giving us another day in which to live.

Psalm 145v2

"Every day I will bless you and praise your name forever and ever"

Each day is a blessing, a gift from above and one we can so easily forget to show gratitude for. Like the child at a birthday party who is so overloaded with gifts that appreciation for yet another one is not forthcoming. And then another gift bearer arrives and by the shape of the present the birthday celebrant knows what is concealed beneath the paper, not something he wants or is excited about. He's in no hurry to open the gift or to express gratitude to the giver.

Maybe you have woken this morning and you are like the child with the birthday gift, you know what the day holds and it is not something to be excited about.

Psalm 145v2

"Every day I will bless you and praise your name forever and ever"

Let's determine before the sun sets this evening to bless Him and praise Him for this day, to not take it for granted no matter how many we have already been given and to open it excitedly even if we know by the shape that it is not something we eagerly anticipate or requested.

Father, thank You for the gift of today. I will bless and praise Your name forever and ever.

Cinderella Moments – Our Father

Daddy, Dad, Da, Papa, Tata, Father, Padre, Pa, some of the names we call our earthly Fathers. Papa, can I? Daddy please help. Pa lift me. Dad what should I do?

Small children have complete faith and trust in their fathers to offer help when required. To take care of their every need and to carry them when weary legs are objecting. Our Father, who art in heaven hallowed be thy name. How much greater should our trust be in our Heavenly Father?

This morning I went for an early morning walk along an empty Spanish beach. The plough was out, cleaning the sand, bringing to light some buried lost belongings. As I passed a family with their metal detector excitedly digging, I thought, that can't find what I lost yesterday.

A sea shoe thrown to me across very wavy waters by my daughter, got picked up by the waves and dragged out. I said a little prayer and claimed Malachi 3v11, that He rebukes the devourer when we tithe.

15 hours later lying at the edge of the waves as I walked along, I spotted my little pink shoe. I said a prayer of thanks to my Heavenly Father. Often it is the seeming insignificant answers to prayer that are most humbling.

Luke 12v29-31

"And do not seek what you will eat and what you will drink, and do not keep worrying. For all these things the nations of the world eagerly seek but your Father knows that you need these things. But seek His kingdom of God and these things shall be added to you".

Whatever Cinderella situation you face this morning, no matter how seemingly insignificant it may seem, you can trust your Heavenly Father for its resolution.

Our Father, who art in heaven, hallowed be thy name.

Sea glass – Smoothing the sharp edges

Who when walking bare foot on soft grains of sand wants to step on a piece of glass hidden under the sand? Sharp, jagged and with the potential to cut and tear.

Many of us will have picked up sea glass. This is admired, collected and even used in works of art and jewellery. Glass whose rough edges have been smoothed out.

Some people can appear like a piece of glass. Cutting with their words and sharp edged if you brush against them.

Ephesians 5v25-28

"Husbands Love your wives, just as Christ loved the church and gave himself up for her to make her holy, cleansing her with the washing of water through the word and to present her to himself as a radiant church without stain or wrinkle or any other blemish, but holy and blameless"

The left behind glass on the beach wasn't transformed overnight, it was a process over time. And when smooth it became useful. So too for the Christian, even those who are mature in the Lord as we spend time in His presence and time in the word. He works on our corners and rough edges, making us smooth.

Heavenly Father, we thank You for washing us with Your word today, smoothing what needs smoothing and making us more pleasant, presentable and productive.

The Opponent – Stay in the fight

He picks up his racquet, throws the ball into the air and serves. Over the net his opponent stands at the ready. Each player wants to win this point. In the corner of the ring stands a boxer. Focused and ready to meet his opponent. Determined to win the next round. Over the net we have an opponent watching our next serve and in the far corner of the ring we have an opponent who would like to take us out. He doesn't wear tennis whites or boxing gloves and certainly doesn't play by the rules. Not only is he interested in winning the next point but game, set and match or the entire fight.

Ephesians 6v12

"But our struggle is not against flesh and blood but against the rulers, against the authorities, against the powers of this dark world and against the spiritual forces of evil in the heavenly realms"

Rather than focusing on the opponent over the net or the one warming up in the far corner. Let's focus on who is serving with us and who is in our corner of the ring. He who enables and equips us, helps us take the next serve and tells us to stay in the ring even when we have lost a round or been knocked to the ground. He says up on your feet, stay in the fight.

For He has already disarmed powers and authorities, triumphing over them by the cross. - Colossians 2v15.

So, when it feels like our opponent is winning every set and each round has gone in his favour. We have to determine to stay on the court and in the ring, knowing that though the afflictions of the righteous may be many, He delivers us out of every one- Psalm 34v19.

And though we may have lost a set or a round we know when the match is over or when the bell summons the end of the fight, who will be doing the victory lap.

2 Corinthians 2v14

"But thanks be to God, who in Christ leads us in triumphal procession and through us spreads the fragrance of the knowledge of Him everywhere"

Father help me to stay on the court and in the ring, even when it looks like the match or the fight isn't going my way. Thank You that though my afflictions may be many, You promise to deliver me out of every one.

Decked Out – Number and suit

The cards tumbled onto the floor of the sleeping aircraft. I scrambled for them before counting. My game of solitaire would be over if the tally wasn't 52. For even the absence of one little card, would put an end to the game.

In the game of life, some have felt like an insignificant card, the one people don't rejoice to be dealt. However, while the trumped ace is the coveted card in a game of whist, if you are a two of clubs and waiting to be picked up by someone whose hand totals 19 in a game of 21 you are a welcomed delight. While a little four of hearts, might be just what the next player needs to finish his run in rummy and crown him the winner.

No matter if you are the King of spades, the 7 of clubs or the 10 of diamonds. You are an important and needed part of the deck.

Whispers on the breeze sometimes try to declare otherwise. They try to cause us to wonder whether we have a part in the deck or to think what could I be needed to do when there are 51 others. Every card, no matter the suit and regardless of its' value helps to make the deck complete.

So, if those lying whispers have been blowing around your ears, you can encourage yourself with the truth of what He says in Jeremiah 1v5 "Before I formed in the womb I knew you, before you were born, I set you apart."

He has a plan, a purpose and a destiny for every member of His deck. Each person wears a different face value but all are required and of great worth.

Isaiah 43v4

"Since you are precious and honoured in my sight and because I love you"

Father help me not to let today slip past without playing my part in Your deck and showing value be it by giving, praying, teaching, serving, witnessing or encouraging. If I have struggled to believe my value, help me to remember that You have a plan for my life. I am precious in Your sight and You love me.

The window boxes – Psalm 1

I was given three lovely window boxes for my birthday in May. They were bursting with colour and vitality and I never tired of admiring them as I came and went. I treated them to TLC and diligently watered them. However, sadly two months later I was pulling out shrivelled dead flowers and brown, burnt foliage and there was very little left in the wicker window boxes.

The intense, prolonged heat was more than the plants could endure. There were days when I was away and they didn't get a drink. With their shallow roots there were no reserves for them to draw from and they struggled to survive.

The trees on the other hand around us are still flourishing in spite of the drought. Their roots go way down deep into the soil.

We have all felt the heat from trials. Some have been short lived and while we didn't like them, we recovered from them quickly. Other trials are more persistent. We may feel like the flowers in my window boxes with the hot sun beating down relentlessly on them for weeks. At times like this we need to dig down deep into our reserves.

Psalm 1V1-3

"Blessed is the man who walks not in the counsel of the ungodly, nor stands in the path of sinners nor sits in the seat of the scornful. But his delight is in the law of the Lord and in His law, he meditates day and night. He shall be like a tree planted by the rivers of water, that brings forth its fruit in its season, whose leaf also shall not wither; and whatever he does shall prosper"

This beautiful, well-known Psalm talks of the man who delights in the law of the Lord, who meditates on it both day and night. This wise man is letting his roots go down deep and then when the heat of a trial burns down and burns down and burns down, he draws from his reserves, put there during cooler seasons and he comes through the heat of the trial and his leaf is not withered and he is still bearing fruit.

In the heat we are forced to drink, we have no choice. On cooler days there is not the same urgency. However, we need to be as diligent to drink from His word on the cool and cold days as we are on the hot, humid, scorching days.

Happy drinking.

Magnified - Praise and Worship

Walking the cliff walk from Bray to Greystones I was sorry we hadn't brought binoculars with us. Looking at something through a magnifying glass or pair of binoculars doesn't change the size of what we are looking at, but it changes our ability to see it. The birds down the cliff wouldn't have been small distant objects, in a sea of blue and green if I had binoculars to look at them with.

Psalm 34v3

"Oh, magnify the Lord with me, let us exalt His name together"

Psalm 69v30

"I will praise the name of God with a song, I will magnify Him with thanksgiving"

We sing songs with children about, "Our God being so big". He never changes in size or ability, but our perception of His size can change. Sometimes it is like looking down the cliff, the birds appear so small compared to the size of the ocean unless we look at them through a magnified lens.

At times, it can appear like the situations we are in, are a vast ocean and we are scrambling to see Him as we ask "where are you Lord?"

As the words of Psalm 69 declare, I will magnify Him with thanksgiving. Praising and worshipping Him corporately or by ourselves is like looking at Him afresh through a magnified lens. It can be an act of faith or obedience to praise and worship when our emotions don't feel like it and situations declare otherwise.

But when we start to praise, worship and offer thanksgiving, the ocean of negative emotion and the sea of situations become smaller and their shout becomes a whisper while God becomes magnified. His voice and His promises shout louder than any negative emotion or situation we are facing.

1 Chronicles 16v23-25

"Sing to the Lord all the earth, proclaim his salvation day after day. Declare his glory among the nations, his marvellous deeds among all the peoples. For great is the Lord and most worthy of praise"

I will sing to the Lord and proclaim His salvation day after day, I will declare His glory among the nations and his marvellous deeds. For great is My Lord and most worthy of praise.

UNO – Be yourself

Heading to Trim castle yesterday. I was reading the road signs pointing to the different places. I spotted some names of places that I know nothing about. If places had feelings, how would they feel? Nestled between the great Meath tourist town of Trim and the well-known Kildare town of Kilcock, could they be tempted to feel overshadowed at times, by places that have seemingly greater importance?

There are many well-known places in Ireland that have different claims to fame be it something of natural beauty, a historic site, great retail opportunities or a sporting venue. Then there are other places that have no seeming significance except to those who reside or work there or whose roots are there.

Are they of any less importance or value? They are part of this land. They have made it onto the map. Sometimes we may be tempted to feel overshadowed by others who are doing acts of seeming greater significance or nobility to us.

Our call is not to do something great or significant, our call is to walk the walk of obedience in the shoes He has given us. It is hard to wear someone else's, they just don't fit right and make walking hard and uncomfortable and the journey unenjoyable.

Oscar Wilde said "be yourself, everyone else is already taken".

There are no significant or more noble in His kingdom, just obedient children.

Father thank You for who You have made me to be. Help me to always be myself, stay true to You and true to myself. Help me to never sign up for or into the comparison game, for there is no winners in that game. But rather help me to play the game of UNO, one me, with a unique call and destiny.

I see you - Integrity

A beautiful summers day spent hiking in the Dublin mountains. The lovely surroundings, shared only with the birds twittering in the purple heather and the butterfly's fluttering past.

We stumbled upon the remains of a disused camp site. There written in bonfire ash on an old log seat were three little words. "I see you". Just when you felt like no one was watching!

I am sure everyone has had the thought at some time "no one can see me" or "no one will ever know".

Integrity is doing the right thing even when no one is watching. It is being able to sleep peacefully, knowing our conscience is clear and that we have chosen to do the right thing even when no one was watching.

Psalm 37v37

"Mark the blameless man and observe the upright, for the future of that man is peace"

Proverbs 11v3

"The integrity of the upright guides them but the crookedness of the treacherous destroys them"

Proverbs 21v3

"To do what is right and just is more acceptable to the Lord than sacrifice"

So even when man isn't watching and listening to us, He is and is saying "I see you".

Father help me to do the right thing, even when no one else is watching. Help me to always chose the path of integrity.

What do I do with this? - Wisdom

Picture someone returning to earth who died one hundred years ago and placing in their hands some of the gadgets we now use on a daily basis. Many of which have made our lives easier and save time. The visitor to earth not only wouldn't know what they were, but wouldn't know what to do with them or their potential benefits.

Many people have knowledge but don't have the wisdom to apply this knowledge. What good is amassing and storing up great knowledge, just for knowledges sake, it has to be applied?

Proverbs 4v7

"Wisdom is the principal thing, therefore get wisdom and in all thy getting, get understanding"

How many times do we face a decision and are unsure what to do? Many have tossed and turned anxiously at night, unable to sleep trying to decide what to do, they have knowledge but need wisdom what to do.

James 1v5

"If any of you lacks wisdom, let him ask of God, who gives to all liberally and without reproach will be given to him"

Therein lies the key, asking Him for wisdom.

Proverbs 2v6

"For the Lord gives wisdom, from His mouth come knowledge and understanding. He stores up sound wisdom for the upright ".

We thank Him for wisdom for all decisions that we face today and the situations we are in.

Proverbs 3v13

"Happy is the man who finds wisdom"

Father when I lack wisdom, may I come and ask of You. I am promised that when I do, that You will give this wisdom liberally to me.

Square peg – Fitting in

Have you heard the saying, "you can't fit a square peg into a round hole"? That is unless you are prepared to get out your tool box and start chiselling and sanding, it's just not going to work.

Have you ever felt like that square peg, who just doesn't seem to fit in certain situations or settings? No amount of sucking in your stomach or holding your breathe will enable your square shaped views or behaviours fit in with the rounder shaped ones of those around you.

We are not called to "fit in" because in some instances that would mean chiselling away at our integrity when asked to do something, we know just isn't right with our "squared" views. We don't want any of our core values sanded away just to make them tolerable to the "round" values, that at times seem to be all around us.

The one we need to "square" our ideas, attitudes, behaviour with is the one who gave us the last breath we took and is giving us the next breath, we will make.

Just because some might like to label certain lifestyles, views and values old fashioned and backward, doesn't mean we get out the chisel and sandpaper. For He calls them righteous.

Matthew 5v15

"Neither do people light a lamp and put it under a bowl. Instead, they put it on a stand and it gives light to everyone in the house"

Let's keep shining our light in this dark world, knowing it is okay to be the square peg at times in a very round world.

Father help me to never be tempted to change my square views, which are in line with Your word, just to fit in with any rounder views around me.

Finish it - **Don't quit**

I sat and watched a group of students kicking a football before the school bell summoned them indoors. One enthusiastically shouted "finish it" to his classmate with the football. Poignant words, given that they were sixth years and when the school bell resounded at 2pm, that is what they had done. Finished their 13 or 14 years of schooling. I am sure there were good days, not so good and those that fell somewhere in between. They celebrated the highs and they kept going on the harder days but they didn't quit and they could hold their heads high on graduation day, knowing they went all the way.

2 Chronicles5v17

"Be strong and do not give up for your work will be rewarded"

Isaiah 41v10

"So do not fear for I am with you, do not be dismayed for I am your God, I will strengthen you and help you, I will uphold you with my righteous right hand"

Sometimes giving up may seem like the thing to do, it may be the logical thing, the easy thing but deep within we hear a little voice saying. "Finish it". There are things we are not to give up on but rather trust Him for strength and He will bring us all the way. Running with us, holding our hand when we need encouragement and carrying us when we feel like we don't have the physical, mental or emotional strength to take even one more step.

Father, thank You for the help and strength to go all the way. To finish what needs to be finished.

Just born – Unconditional love

The tiny, new born baby is carefully placed into their parents' arms. The overwhelming emotion the parents feel when looking at the little face and into the just opened eyes is love. Deep unconditional love. There are many thoughts racing through their heads of awe and wonder, but equally there are many things they are not thinking in this moment.

No mental note to self is being penned in the parent's head, titled "conditions to my love". In their minds eye they are not busy writing "My baby's first to do list". When you have smiled twice and gurgled four times, slept through the night for a week, then I will love you. There is no forward planning going on and job lists written for each year. When you have washed 100 plates, swept many floors and tidied countless toy boxes then I will love□ you. Neither is the parent thinking of the achievements their tiny new born must accomplish in order to merit their love. Be that to win first prize in the beautiful baby competition, to have the cutest smile or to be the fastest crawler in the baby group. They just love this little baby without that child having to do anything to earn or merit it.

Romans 5v 8

"God shows His love for us that while we were still sinners, he died for us"

We did nothing to merit or earn our Heavenly Fathers love and we need to remain confident in this love through every season and not slip into secular ways of thinking. If I could do more in the kingdom or if I could achieve more then He would surely love me more. Or I would be more entitled to my heavenly Fathers love.

If feelings of being unloved or unlovable try to slither into our heads, we can deny them entry. If we are constantly striving to do more and achieve more, we can stop and remember you are loved by love itself.

1 John 4v7

"Dear friends let us love one another for love comes from God, whoever loves has been born again and knows God. Whoever does not love does not know God because God is Love"

Take out your deck chair and bask in the heat of that love today.

Father, thank You that you loved first. Thank you for your unconditional, unmerited love.

Stony walk – Casting the cares

Have you ever walked and shared your shoe with a pebble? Even the tiniest one can hamper your progress. No matter the thickness of your sock or the quality of your shoe, they can't protect you from the uninvited guest. You hobble, hop or walk slowly along until you are able to get rid of the pebble.

Some of us are walking with a pebble or many pebbles in our shoes today. They go with us no matter which direction we take and are slowing us down. Now to another person they may appear almost invisible they are so minuscule but we are the one trying to walk with them in our shoe.

We need to unlace, unbuckle or slip off the shoe, locate the pebble and cast the care of it unto the Lord for He cares for us. He tells us in Matthew not to worry about tomorrow. So often a pebble we are carrying is to do with tomorrow or next week or next year and that pebble is stopping us enjoying the now, it is preventing us doing what we should be doing today.

In Philippines 4 it tells us not to worry about anything but rather instead to pray about everything. Turn those pebbles into prayers and your steps will become lighter and we are promised in verse 7 of the same chapter that the peace of God which transcends all understanding will guard our hearts and minds in Christ Jesus.

Philippians 4v6&7

"Be anxious about for nothing, but in everything by prayer and supplication with thanksgiving, let your requests be made known to God, and the peace of God, which surpasses all understanding, will guard your hearts and minds through Christ Jesus"

Happy pebble throwing today.

Keep running! – Being an encourager

I stood on the East link bridge helping steward at a night run. Blue sirens in the distance signalled the lead runner was approaching. He glided past at ease as did those who were close behind him. There were thousands running behind the Kenyan out front. Very little sound could be heard save for the pounding of feet on the road and some laboured breathing.

I spotted the police man near me, clapping just on two occasions, that was for the two men pushing another before them. We live in an age where the television screens shout "you have to be a winner" or face elimination. This is across the board in music, talent, cookery, the arts and the list goes on and on.

God isn't looking for those who simply want to outwit and beat another. He is looking for those who will run their race, all the way to the finish. In His race the fastest runner will get a prize but equally those way down the back who have to exert great determination and effort to make it all the way. Some in the night run took breaks from running and walked when the going got tough but they kept moving. We are told in Corinthians that the winner of a race wins a perishable crown, but we are running for imperishable crowns.

I, a spectator was asked was I considering taking up running. There are those who watch from the side lines, some unsure, some undecided but who need encouragement to join the race, that will not end not at a finish tape but at heavens gates.

As we run, there are times when those around us need encouragement. I listened to a man near the back of the field of runners shouting encouragement to those alongside him. There are other times when some need carrying. Our focus shouldn't be simply on what we want to achieve in our race but also on helping others to make it across the finish line.

We are told in Hebrews to run with endurance the race that is set before us. As we go, we need to keep our eyes and ears open attentive for the cries of one who needs encouraging or carrying today.

Father help me to run my race to the finish and as I run, help me to be aware of the needs of those who are running around me. Help me to be ready to encourage, support and to carry. Help me to be sensitive to those who have more to overcome to make it to the finish tape, more hurdles to jump than I have, obstacles to go around.

Not even a peek – Run from it

Last night something started to play on playback. It was part of a teaching that I gave at a youth retreat a couple of months ago. I know some reading this today may not fall into the youth category but don't be tempted to change the channel or switch the off button. There was a young salmon named Sammy who was born and reared in the river Liffey. He lived a contented life but as he grew so did his desire for freedom and greater independence. Finally, his mother agreed he was now old enough to swim solo. As she waved him off on his first adventure she said, "son, please heed this one piece of advice. Eat well on your travels have fun but avoid any piece of food that seems to shine and shimmer". He took his mother's advice to heart, flicked his tail and off he went. It wasn't long before he spotted a worm dangling right in his path. A fatter, pinker or juicier worm he had never seen before and his little heart fluttered with excitement. But, when he got close to it, his mother's parting words rang in his ears for the worm seemed to shimmer and sparkle.

What harm he thought, I will have a tiny taste, a mere lick. This was his plan and his intention. However, such a tasty worm had never before he tasted so back out of the reeds he swam and back over, just for a nibble. Sheer delight. Unfortunately, though neither the lick nor the nibble had satisfied his hunger but rather had given him an appetite for more. So back he swam telling himself he would take one big bite and off home he would go and no one would ever be any the wiser that he hadn't followed his mother's advice. He opened his little fish mouth as wide as he could, desire fuelled by a hunger for more and then slammed his mouth closed. Pain ripped through his mouth. He wriggled, writhed and twisted but he was stuck. Not free to go where he wanted to go. He had been hooked.

In Proverbs it tells us, if sinners entice you. One version says turn your back on them, another says do not consent and a third one says do not give in to them. In 1 Corinthians 6v18 we are told to flee from sexual immorality. We could take that verb flee and apply it to many other areas too. 2 Timothy 2v22 says to flee youthful lusts. Poor Sammy Salmon should have listened to the wisdom of his mother and should have fled at speed when he saw that the worm sparkled because the first taste didn't satisfy, it simply gave him a hunger for more until eventually he became hooked and trapped. We thank God that we have a saviour who is always ready when we make a wrong turn to shout loudly wrong way, turn back. We have a loving Father who stands ready to cut us out of any messes and tangles we have got ourselves into. Thank God we serve the God of the second chance and the third and the fourth. So even if we have messed up like Sammy, He stands ready to forgive us and to set us back on the right path.

Tug of War – The next generation

After hearing a little promo on the radio about a tug of war it made me think, about young people. The next generation of children, teenagers and young adults. Picture them for a minute and the little marker on the tug of war rope, as they are pulled between two kingdoms. Today let's pick up the tug of war rope for the young people in our circle of influence. Our children and grandchildren, nieces, nephews, friends' children, young people in our church and in our community.

Let's pick up their ropes alongside them and tug the rope in prayer. Pick up the rope and be a Godly example in the affairs of life. Modelling faithfulness and integrity, being an example in love and compassion, showing empathy and walking in forgiveness. Let's take the rope in our palms and reach out to these young people in love and encouragement and as we tug let us shout loudly. Yes, very loudly to be heard above all the voices on the other side of the rope that are vying for their attention. Remind them of the words in Jeremiah that God has a plan for their life.

Jeremiah 29v11

"For I know the plans I have for you" declares the Lord, "plans to prosper you and not to harm you, plans to give you hope and a future""

Tell them that Psalm 119 teaches that the way a young man keeps himself pure is by living according to God's word.

Psalm 119v9

"How can a young person stay on the path of purity? By living according to your word"

In this day when you can be made believe that you must look beautiful or handsome without a hair out of place 24/7 and 365 days of the year, remind them that they are uniquely crafted, fearfully and wonderfully made and what is in the packet is of far more value than the packaging itself.

Psalm 139v14

"I praise you for I am fearfully and wonderfully made"

Father help me to do my part for the next generation by praying, reaching out, being a good role model, encouraging and when You lead by ministering to them.

Running the aisles - **Our gifts**

Picture a small child in a large toy shop. They run the aisles excitedly. They look, they touch, they talk about what they would like. Toys are chosen, paid for and brought home. But then rather than being allowed to open the packaging, they are wrapped in wrapping paper and put in a gift bag. The toy is a gift for someone else. The young child cries and pleads with their parents to keep it. They don't want to give it. But it was never there's in the first place, it was a gift to benefit someone else.

In 1 Peter it says God has given each one of us a gift.

I Peter 4v10&11

"God has given each of you a gift from his great variety of spiritual gifts. Use them well to serve one another. Do you have the gift of speaking? Then speak as though God himself were speaking through you. Do you have the gift of helping others? Do it with all the strength and energy that God supplies. Then everything you do will bring glory to God through Jesus Christ"

This verse tells us to use our God given gifts to serve one another. A gift is not for the bearer but for the recipient. If the small child refuses to give the gift, his friend or family member loses out. We can all think of many reasons and excuses not to use our God given gift. Lack of time, lack of confidence, shyness, insecurities, past failures and the list goes on.

But we need to remember it's a gift to benefit others. And in using our gifts we ourselves will benefit from a great sense of fulfilment. The wise parent of the young child won't allow them to hold onto the present from the toy store. But will sit their child down and give them a lesson on giving, on kindness and on thinking of others. Likewise, our heavenly Father pushes and urges us to never get overly comfortable but to press on and push on in using our God given gifts.

Father thank You for the gifts that You have entrusted me with.

The skyscraper – Taste and see

Picture someone on the top floor of a sky scraper. They are feeling on top of the world. Until… Something happens. It may be an interaction with a colleague or harsh words from a family member. They may get a telephone call, an email or correspondence in the post. Whatever it is, it sees them running out the door and hoping into the lift. Very quickly they are on the way down. As they descend, they stop at different floors picking up some companions. It doesn't take long to reach the dark, gloomy basement, far from the panoramic views where they started off. Looking out, looking forward and feeling excited. We can all be like that person in the sky scraper when bad news comes or something happens that annoys or upsets us. But what we should keep our focus on is He who is never changing.

Hebrews 13v8

"Jesus Christ is the same yesterday, today and forever"

No matter what comes our way, it doesn't change Him. The person in the dingy basement needs to wrestle his travelling companions out of the lift. Perhaps fear joined him in the lift, or the interaction may have caused anger to jump in at floor ten. Self-pity pressed the button on level three and jealousy jumped in on the ground floor. Some eviction orders need to be given. Once the weights are gone, his ascent becomes easier. The book of Psalms is a great reminder of the character of our Heavenly Father as well as His ability no matter, the situation we face.

Psalm 27v1

"The Lord is my light and my salvation – whom shall, I fear? The Lord is the stronghold of my life – of whom shall I be afraid?"

Psalm 29v11

"The Lord gives strength to his people; the Lord blesses his people with peace"

As the person in the lift, starts to raise their voice in praise and concentrates on Him, the lift moves up from the dimly lit basement. Before long he is back up at the top of the skyscraper and is determined the next time things don't go his way not to run so fast to the lift. We don't want to be living life in a permanent elevator flying up and down as circumstances dictate but rather, we can be grounded on Him.

Psalm 108v1 "My heart is steadfast, O God, I will sing and make music with all my soul".

Home Fed – Grateful for those who feed us

Walking the dog on a beautiful warm, Monday morning. I remembered at last to bring a little container to pick blackberries. As I walked, I tried to pick some berries which were in sparse supply while hanging onto a dog who had more interest in hunting squirrels than berries. When I got back to the car, hanging over the stone wall right beside it, were clumps of big, juicy berries, that the weekend scavengers had overlooked. They were so ripe they fell off the branches and into my container. I hadn't needed to go anywhere to fill my container.

It made me think how we as Christians get fed. Sometimes we go online, drive or even take a plane☐ in search of a powerful word. There is a time and a place for all that but let's not forget the "home feeding" which we get in our own home churches.

Think of a child, the majority of their dining will be at home, food prepared by a parent/guardian. Occasionally they will eat a takeout or in a restaurant and at other times they will be invited to friends/family to dine. But most of their nourishment will be around their own table. Sometimes a parent may serve food that is nourishing but not to the child's taste but the parent knows their nutritional needs.

Today let's take a moment to thank God for those who feed us spiritually on a regular basis. They know what was on the menu last week and know what is planned up ahead and they know what is beneficial for us to be served today. Let's, pray for the men and women of God who tirelessly feed us around our church tables, week in and week out. Let's show gratitude and appreciation to these men and women for what they have prepared and served us and not be too quick to race over to tell them the great offerings that are being served down the road, across town or online.

Father help me not to over look the "home feeding." Help me to show gratitude towards those who prepare and serve it.

Remorse - **Regret**

I asked the Lord what to write and I heard one word. Remorse. A couple of years ago I was in bed when the Lord started to speak to me for a friend about regret. He started to give me a story on the topic. I didn't want to forget it while I slept so I jumped out of bed and stumbled in the dark into my daughter's room on a pen finding mission. Suddenly pain shot through my leg and another mission began, that being to pray for my leg. I had stood on something in the dark.

I lay in bed in pain and kept thinking, Oh God why didn't I just turn on a light. Over and over the thought came. My birthday was the next day and I had plans and now wondered would they be able to be fulfilled. The record played on "why didn't I turn on the light". It struck me that no matter how many times I thought this particular thought the outcome was going to be the same. A sore foot. I got a practical example for the regret story I was about to pen.

The old record called regret slips very easily onto the record player at times but listening to it doesn't benefit us. Regret is such a useless emotion.

Philippians 3v13

"One thing I do forgetting what lies behind and straining forward to what lies ahead. I press on toward the goal for the prize of the upward call of God in Christ Jesus"

I switched off the record player and prayed. The day of another birthday to be celebrated dawned and I was able to fulfil and enjoy what had been planned and another lesson learnt on the way.

Father help me today to say goodbye to regret. Help me to see it for what it is. I choose to lay down regrets for things I did or said that I shouldn't have and for those things which I wish I had done or said but didn't. I choose to forget what lies behind and strain forward to what lies ahead.

Propped up – Support & Encouragement

I spotted a bicycle propped up in Trinity college this morning. The old-fashioned black bike with the basket was leaning against a pillar. Remove the pillar and the bicycle would go crashing down. It needs the pillar to offer support and to hold it up. There are times we feel like the bicycle, in need of another for support or to prop us up. Then there are times when we are the pillar offering support to someone in need.

I got a letter in the post this week, handwritten envelope indicated something desirable inside. Encouragement dripped off the page from my cousin and how good it felt to read it, which I did multiple times. I hadn't told my cousin how I was feeling, but I had told Him.

1 Thessalonians 5v11

"Therefore encourage one another and build each other up"

How easy it is to encourage another, yet we can so often let the busyness of our own lives and schedules get in the way.

Galatians 6v2, tells us to bear one another's burdens. The pillar in Trinity bore the weight of the bicycle. There are times when those around us face trials, situations, circumstances that are very heavy to bear and they need us to help with their burdens, lifting them up in prayer, providing a listening ear, showing support and love in practical ways and being there for them to lean on until they are able to do without it. We are told in Thessalonians 5 to "encourage the fainthearted and help the weak", the NIV says to "encourage the disheartened".

Proverbs 12v25

"Anxiety weighs down the heart, but a kind word cheers it up"

My prayer today for the reader is that if you feel like the bicycle about to topple over, that the Lord will put you on someone's heart who can pray for you or with you, encourage you with the word, listen if you feel like talking, offer practical support and advise and be a pillar of support for you to lean on.

For those who are strong and not in need of support today, I pray God will give you opportunities to be a pillar of love, support and encouragement to someone else. You may be the answer to someone's prayer.

Cool down – Don't let the sun go down

The day was hot. The sun beat down and we felt it. I watched people taking to the water to cool down. Small children paddled at the water's edge, others swam while the bravest jumped or dived into the icy sea. In the evening my daughter and cousins paddled in the river to cool down hot feet. Sometimes it's not our flesh that burns but our emotions. Like a fire blazing on the inside of us. Many people say when the sun is shining strongly "I can't think straight in this heat". Likewise, when anger or rage burns within a man they can't think straight. We would be well served to take steps like those who took to the waters, to cool down our emotions.

Ephesians 4v26&27

"In your anger do not sin. Do not let the sun go down while you are still angry and do not give the devil a foothold"

Proverbs 29v11

"Fools give full vent to their rage but the wise bring calm in the end"

While the flesh is appeased when it vents the anger that burns within, the above verses say that while a fool vents their anger, a wise person calms themselves down. When we feel the fire of anger blazing within, we need to be like those on the hot day who actively took steps to cool down. As it says in Ephesians 4, we need not let anger cause us to sin.

In Galatians, the fruit of the spirit are listed, one being self-control. Perhaps we have swallowed the lie that we will never be able to control our angr or we come from an angry brood. Perhaps modelled to you growing up was anger, it was all you knew. There is a better and a more pleasant way and one that doesn't leave a trail of destruction in its wake.

James 1v19,20

"My dear brothers and sisters take note of this. Everyone should be quick to listen, slow to speak and slow to become angry because human anger does not produce the righteousness that God desires".

Next time you feel that flame of anger starting to alight within you, go paddle, swim, or jump and cool down before you speak, react or act.

Father I repent for any past angry outbursts. Help me to not sin in anger and to not let the sun go down on my wrath. If amends need to be made for things said or done in anger, please help me begin that process.

Jam preferences – Standing still

I am sure if asked we would all have different jam preferences. On the other hand, I'm sure most share a common distaste for the same flavour of jam, the one that puts your plans on hold, delays you and can cause frustration. That being the traffic Jam.

Have you ever found yourself sitting on a motorway, with all lanes blocked? Then the lane to your left begins moving, soon after the one to the right of you moves. You, on the other hand remain static staring at the break lights of the vehicle in front of you.

Have you ever felt as if your journey with the Lord has come to an unexpected and unscheduled stand still? You sit trying to keep frustration at bay while wondering why those in the lane to the left of you are seeing answered prayers and great personal breakthrough and those in the right lane are getting great opportunities to use their gifts and talents.

Some in standstill traffic jams have taken detours. Little did they know that as soon as they exited the motorway, their lane started to move freely again.

We serve a God of the suddenly.

1 Samuel 12v16

"Now then stand still and see this great thing the Lord is about to do before your eyes"

2 Chronicles 20v17

"You will not even need to fight. Take your position then stand still and watch the Lord's victory"

Sometimes, the hardest thing to do is to do nothing. Such effort is required to do absolutely nothing except, stand still. However, this is sometimes exactly what we need to do, simply stand still and wait, with listening ears, watching eyes attentive and expectant for the lane up ahead to start moving again. We want to be in the right place when that happens and not off on some rabbit trail of a detour.

Father if that is me, sitting in a lane of traffic that appears blocked, waiting for the traffic to move. Help me to take my position, stand still and let You bring victory, in Jesus' name.

What will I be? - Serving

If a teacher asks their class of seven-year-olds what they want to be when they grow up, the answers though different will probably follow a common thread. Anything is seen as possible, for most seven-year-olds don't see the limitations of exam results, college places or their own abilities/inabilities.

The teacher would hear dreams among others I am sure, of being pilots, doctors, nurses and designers. Would any pupil express a desire to be a servant?

What image does the word servant conjure up in your mind? I think of times past when many entered domestic service and served the owners of fine dwellings.

The word "servant" can have negative connotations. Yet the words of a children's song say "if you want to be great in God's kingdom, you gotta be the servant of all". Something which goes against worldly wisdom.

Mark 10v45

"For the son of man did not come to be served but to serve and give His life as a ransom for many"

We are called to have the heart of a servant, in our homes, communities and churches. We are told in Luke "that the one who is greatest must become like the youngest and the leader like the servant".

The true mark of greatness is to have humble servant's heart. A desire to serve, rather than be served, not for self-gain but rather to bless those we share homes with, our community and the Kingdom with.

Father thank You for those who have enriched my life with their servants' hearts. Please help me to enrich and bless the lives of others by having a servant's heart. Let the cry of my heart be not to be served but to serve others.

The hard part – **In His presence**

The "hard part" that was the heading that I had accidentally skipped when tye dying a t-shirt for someone. It entails leaving the t-shirt for 24 hours once the dye has been applied. This enables the dye to bond with the fabric.

The end result was that the t-shirt looked washed out, the dye hardly visible. The next t-shirt I left soaking for 24 hours, the dye left its imprint, the colours on the t-shirt, bright and vibrant. Nobody is in any doubt that the once white t-shirt has had prolonged seeping in dye.

In Exodus 34 we read that when Moses came down from Mount Sinai where he had been alone with the Lord, his face was radiant.

V30 "When Aaron and all the Israelites saw Moses, his face was radiant, and they were afraid to come near him"

Spending time in God's presence changes us. It changes our mood, changes our attitudes, changes our outlooks, changes how we feel, changes our behaviour. Those we come into contact with like Aaron and the Israelites with Moses, should be able to tell we have spent time in the presence of the Lord.

Father help me not to be too rushed to come into Your presence and once there help me to settle and not be in a hurry to leave so that when I do Your imprint is on my life. Those I come into contact with can then tell I have spent time in the presence of the Lord.

Puddles – All things work together for good

Small wellington clad feet charge through them sending muddy water splashing. To our dog, finding them is like discovering treasure, drinking from them cools a dry throat and on a cold morning the excitement of cracking the ice on them and crunching it provides great entertainment for her. Puddles, what is deposited by the rain and left long after it passes.

Rain, what few except farmers and those looking for an excuse to stay indoors get excited by in this country. Yet, we all appreciate its effects. The rain passes and leaves the puddles for the thirsty dogs to drink from or children to splash through.

Romans 8v28

"All things work together for good to them that love God to them who are the called according to His purpose"

We have all walked or are walking through some rain, gentle showers and heavy downpours. When the rain has stopped and we have dried off, we need to stop and reflect. Sometimes these rain showers have given us puddles to enjoy, things that wouldn't have happened if it were not for the rain and for this, we are grateful. In addition, like the rain filling up the puddles, the test and trials deposit things in us - patience as we await them to pass, perseverance as we walk through them. Sometimes while walking through the showers and downpours, people have been brought into our lives who we might not have otherwise met.

So, while we don't go looking for or chasing after rain, when we find ourselves caught in a shower let's take time to thank God for what is being deposited in us as we wait for it to pass and the unexpected puddles it leaves long after it has gone.

Father help me to see and appreciate any puddles that have been deposited by the rain which has fallen over and around me.

Judged – Judging another

My attention was drawn to the person speaking loudly to her companion, I soon realized that was the intention.

Up the supermarket aisle they came after me. Should I speak up, speak out, plead guilty, defend myself, fight my corner? Tell them that it was simply an oversight leaving the fridge door open, explain my motive was not to cause the contents of the fridge to sour, tell them where I normally shop the doors close by themselves? I said nothing but simply said "Father I forgive her, bless her."

My actions had been judged. And I reflected how at times I have been the one doing the judging instead of showing mercy for the misdemeanour of a stranger or a loved one. We can often judge a motive rather than allowing someone explain their reason for saying or doing something.

Matthew 7v1-2

"Do not judge, or you too will be judged. For in the same way, you judge others, you will be judged, and with the measure you use, it will be measured to you."

Many times, it can be a relief to off load, get off one's chest, give a piece of one's mind, stare and glare and show disapproval. Often it doesn't stop there, others are told about it, the experience is posted on social media, bad reviews are given and a person's character is shredded or a ministry or business bashed.

And yet the scripture says the measure we use to judge others, will be used against us.

Matthew 5v7

"Blessed are the merciful for they shall be shown mercy"

Father, please bring to mind anyone I have judged. I repent for judging. Please forgive me. Help me to not be so quick to judge but rather to show mercy and to pray instead.

Along the way - Encouragement

I listened to the presenter on a Christian radio station talking about standing at the finish line of a race to offer support to the athletes. He had a light bulb moment. It's not at the end of a race, that a runner needs encouragement but rather "along the way".

Each one of us needs "along the way" encouragement in our race of life. You may be lying on the footpath today, after taking a tumble and need an outstretched hand to pull you back onto your feet again. A fellow runner, may have tripped you up and you not only carry bruises externally but are stinging from the injustice of the situation.

Perhaps you feel parched and need a cool drink passed to you. Or you may simply ache all over from the length of the race, and a shout or cheer can help spur you on towards the finish line.

There are times our "along the way" encouragement comes beautifully gift wrapped. We eagerly unwrap the package to discover tissues to catch the tears and the gift bearer stands ready with soothing words and a hug.

However, on other occasions we need a different approach to get us back up and running. For sometimes, we have sat too long on the curb, by the roadside nursing our woes. We need to hear words like a mother would say to a small child "you're fine, dry those eyes and off you run". If our encouragement comes in this way, we need to receive it and not shoot the giver down or take offence feeling they are lacking in compassion or are being too hard on us or insensitive to our situation.

At other times our encouragement parcel is full of tools. Don't throw them aside and hope someone else will fix the situation for you. For sometimes what is required to get us running again is wisdom and the gift comes with practical advice. Let's not be quick to say "that won't work' or "tried that before and it's pointless".

Father I pray for those who are sitting or lying by the roadside in need of encouragement. I pray that You will send whatever is required to get them back up on their feet and running in the race. And Lord for those who don't need encouragement I pray that You will send them across another's path as a source of encouragement and exhortation.

1 Thessalonians 5v11 says "therefore comfort each other and edify one another."

Never too late – Salvation of loved one

A traffic jam on our road on a Saturday morning was an unusual sight and not only that, but the steady procession of people walking up and down the road made exiting the gate difficult.

It was Election Day, and the polling station is situated in the school at the top of our road. I could be tempted to panic and think "I better get there quickly and early like everyone else and vote". Even though I had planned to go that night with the other voting members of my family.

The vote cast at 7am by the organized, early bird has no greater weight than that cast by someone flying in the door at the very last minute and casting their vote at 10pm.

There are those raised in Christian homes or attending Christian schools or with Christian grandparents who hear the gospel message at a young age, so they are like the 7 am voters many making a decision for Christ early in their lives.

Then there are others who right at the last minute, just before they leave this earth make a decision for Christ. Like the 10pm voter, who just made it in the doors before the polling station closed, their vote still counts.

We need to take heart, there may be loved ones who have resisted the gospel message and they are in the twilight seasons of their live's. The devils' whispers can be heard in the night declaring "it is too late".

We need to not grow weary in praying for family, friends, neighbours and colleagues even if they appear resistant to the gospel message, trusting that even at the very last minute, they can cry out to the Lord. That cry is just as effective as the earnest prayer of the three year old child inviting Jesus into their heart.

Revelation 3v20

"Behold I stand at the door and knock, if anyone hears my voice and opens the door, I will come into him"

Lord help me to keep praying for loved ones, neighbours, colleagues, acquaintances that don't yet know You. Help me to keep trusting and keep sowing seed even if there appears to be nothing happening in the natural.

Sticks & Stones – Harsh words

"Sticks and stones may break your bones but words will never hurt you." Bumps, thumps, breaks, knocks, bruises and cuts all heal over time and minor ones tend to be soon forgotten about. Yet words have the ability to resurface, even words spoken from our childhood. Many people will say "a teacher told me that I would…" "my father said I was…" "my mother called me a ..." Unfortunately, it's often the critical words that stay with us, sometimes even after the person who spoke them is dead.

Psalm 127v3-5

"Behold, children are a heritage from the Lord, the fruit of the womb is a reward. Like arrows in the hand of a warrior, so are the children of one's youth. Happy is the man who has his quiver full of them"

This verse tells us, children are a heritage from the Lord, a reward and those who have a quiver full of them are happy or some versions say blessed. Unfortunately for some, they were not made to believe they were a reward or a heritage but may have heard "unwanted" or "unplanned" and concluded they were "unwelcome".

Jeremiah 1v5

"Before I formed you in the womb, I knew you; before you were born, I sanctified you; I ordained you a prophet to the nations"

Just as He said to Jeremiah, He could say the same to each one of us. He knew us before we were born and had a plan for each of our lives. Some reading this may have been told "you will never", "you will always be". Some were called cruel things by peers and while the rhyme at the start says words don't hurt, we all know the contrary is the truth. Some children or teenagers even heard the words - "a waste of space". Words spoken hastily, words spoken without thought, words spoken in anger, little seeds which fell on the fertile soil of a young person's heart and started to put down roots. Little shoots grew and produced fruit. For some it may be time to get out the shovel and dig up some "weed words". Even if the speaker of those words is no longer in your life or now deceased. Hard as it can be, we can make a decision to release those who spoke the words. Forgiveness doesn't justify the offense but it frees us from the effects.

Father help me to forgive those who spoke words that they shouldn't to me or in my hearing. Please heal the pain caused by those words. Help me to plant new seeds by reading and mediating on the truths from Your word, for I am *"Fearfully and wonderfully made."*

Don't get stuck in it – Love covers

One thing you are guaranteed driving on Irish roads is that sooner or later you will meet a pot hole. Sometimes we can swerve our way around them while on other occasions we find ourselves driving right through them.

Luke 17v1

"Jesus said to his disciples, 'it is impossible that no offenses will come"

This verse tells us that like potholes on Irish roads, offenses are guaranteed. Some we can see in advance and swerve around, while others we find ourselves driving through. A deep pothole can cause damage to our car. So too can offense to us.

At times we have been wronged by another, while on other occasions it is simply a perceived injustice, but we have still been offended by it. The longer we remain in the pothole of offense the more it affects us.

Rather than dealing with it straight away, at times we have cultivated it. We have watered it by dwelling on it, and fed it by telling anyone who will give ear to our issue. It has caused other things to sprout and take root in our hearts, unforgiveness perhaps or bitterness, anger or resentment.

Whether we are justified or not to feel the way we do. Like the car stuck in the very deep pothole unable to move until assistance comes. We are going nowhere until we get rid of the offense.

Proverbs 17v9

"Whoever fosters love, covers over an offense"

Mark 11v25

"Whenever you stand praying, forgive if you have anything against anyone so that your Father who is in heaven may also forgive you your transgressions"

Father today please show me if I have offense in my heart towards an individual, a church, a government, school or work place. Help me to forgive those who caused the offense to come and let reconciliation and healing begin today.

This is my story - Praising

I love these song lyrics.
This is my story,
This is my song
Praising my Saviour all the day long.

We are all writing the stories of our lives. Some have many chapters completed while younger ones are only starting their books. What song are you singing in the current chapter of your life? Are you singing a song of praise and thanksgiving, while doing a victory dance?

Isaiah 63v7

"I will tell of the kindnesses of the LORD, the deeds for which he is to be praised, according to all the LORD has done for us, yes, the many good things"

Perhaps a different song is being sung as you are in a chapter "of yet praising Him", where your praise is sacrificial.

Psalm 42v11

"Why, my soul, are you downcast? Why so disturbed within me? Put your hope in God for I will yet praise him, my Saviour and my God"

It's easy to praise Him from the mountain top but do we still have a song in the valley or when the storm is raging, in times of brokenness, heartache and despair, when we are in the waiting room for a prolonged period and when we can feel the flames from the fiery trial licking around us?

Its' rhythm is trust, the melody is dependence, the pitch is hope and the beat is perseverance. Paul and Silas were in prison, shackled and with none of the comforts or entitlements of some prisons today. But we read that they were praying and singing praises. They hadn't lost their song.

Acts 16v25

"About midnight Paul and Silas were praying and singing hymns to God and the other prisoners were listening to them"

So, no matter whether we find ourself today on the mountain top, in the valley below or clinging desperately to the cliff face, let's keep singing our song of worship to Him, we can praise Him.

Douse it, don't stoke it – A soft answer

The night I inadvertently threw a battery, that was concealed in the bottom of the turf basket into the fire, it caused a mini explosion. At other times when I have been over enthusiastic about burning papers, I have watched the fire roar as the flames lick high up the chimney.

James 3v6

"The tongue also is a fire"

Our words, like the battery in our grate can cause the hearer to explode in anger or to roar like an angry fire. While at times we can feel justified to say what we want to say, in the manner and tone we want to use, doing so could be compared to taking a poker and stoking the fire. Or fanning the flames that are before us. While it may bring short term relief to 'let rip", we need to consider the results. In the morning all that remains in our grate is dirty black ash. We don't want a fiery tongue to cause damage or burn up completely a wholesome relationship.

When in the scouts we were taught not only how to light a camp fire but also how to safely extinguish a fire by dousing it with buckets of river water and then stamping on any remaining embers.

Proverbs 15v1 – Amplified

"A soft and gentle and thoughtful answer turns away wrath. But harsh and painful and careless words stir up anger"

Sometimes we need to be like that scout and instead of fuelling and fanning a fire, we need to douse it with soft words, stamp out any angry flames thus preventing them from spreading.

James 3v5

"Consider what a great forest is set on fire by a small spark"

When the ground is very dry, all it takes is a tiny spark to cause a destructive, roaring fire.

Father today please help us to put away the pokers and not be tempted to stoke any fires with our words but instead help us to douse any combustible situations by choosing to give soft, gentle and thoughtful answers.

I want it now – Waiting patiently

When a new born baby is hungry, they have only one way of letting their care giver know. Their cry is such that lets them know "I'm hungry and I want it now".

There is no point trying to explain that you are in the middle of cooking or have just sat down and want to eat a hot meal. They won't be soothed by being sung a lullaby or a rattle waved in their face won't stop the tears. They want food and "they want it now".

As a child grows, they learn that sometimes they have to wait. Sometimes we can be like the new born "God I want x,y,z and I want it now". Of course, we don't say it using those words. We are much more diplomatic but when translated it simply means "I want it now or why hasn't it happened for me yet?"

God in His wisdom and sovereignty sometimes says - "not yet". The new born baby doesn't like to have to wait to be fed neither does an older child like to be told "not yet" to their question, "is dinner ready". And if we are honest sometimes, we don't like to have to wait.

Psalm 31v15

"My times are in your hands".

Father help us to be patient as we sit in the waiting room and wait.

Psalm 40v1

"I waited patiently for the Lord and He inclined unto me and heard my cry".

Romans 5v4,5

"And patience produces character and character produces hope. And this hope will never disappoint us, because God has poured out His love to fill our hearts"

We thank God that patience is doing a work in us and that any frustration melts away as we put our trust in Him and our hope is restored.

176

My prayer for you the reader is that as you read these devotions, seeds of hope were planted in your heart. May these seeds of hope now be watered, may they grow and may they produce a harvest.

I pray you have been encouraged.

Kate

Printed in Poland
by Amazon Fulfillment
Poland Sp. z o.o., Wrocław

16856361R00105